PRIVACY AND THE INTERNET: YOUR EXPECTATIONS AND RIGHTS UNDER THE LAW

by
Margaret C. Jasper

Oceana's Legal Almanac Series:
Law for the Layperson

2003
Oceana Publications, Inc.
Dobbs Ferry, New York

Information contained in this work has been obtained by Oceana Publications from sources believed to be reliable. However, neither the Publisher nor its authors guarantee the accuracy or completeness of any information published herein, and neither Oceana nor its authors shall be responsible for any errors, omissions or damages arising from the use of this information. This work is published with the understanding that Oceana and its authors are supplying information, but are not attempting to render legal or other professional services. If such services are required, the assistance of an appropriate professional should be sought.

You may order this or any Oceana publication by visiting Oceana's website at http://www.oceanalaw.com or contacting Customer Service at 1.914.693.8100 (domestic or international) or 1.800.831.0758 (U.S. only).

Library of Congress Control Number: 2003108245

ISBN: 0-379-11375-9

Oceana's Legal Almanac Series: Law for the Layperson

ISSN 1075-7376

©2003 by Oceana Publications, Inc.

Manufactured in the United States of America on acid-free paper.

To My Husband Chris

Your love and support
are my motivation and inspiration

-and-

In memory of my son, Jimmy

Table of Contents

CHAPTER 3:
E-MAIL

CHAPTER 4:
E-COMMERCE

CHAPTER 5:
PRIVACY STATEMENTS

CHAPTER 6:
ONLINE FINANCIAL SERVICES

CHAPTER 7:
PROTECTING CHILDREN'S PRIVACY ONLINE

APPENDICES

ABOUT THE AUTHOR

MARGARET C. JASPER is an attorney engaged in the general practice of law in South Salem, New York, concentrating in the areas of personal injury and entertainment law. Ms. Jasper holds a Juris Doctor degree from Pace University School of Law, White Plains, New York, is a member of the New York and Connecticut bars, and is certified to practice before the United States District Courts for the Southern and Eastern Districts of New York, the United States Court of Appeals for the Second Circuit, and the United States Supreme Court.

Ms. Jasper has been appointed to the panel of arbitrators of the American Arbitration Association and the law guardian panel for the Family Court of the State of New York, is a member of the Association of Trial Lawyers of America, and is a New York State licensed real estate broker and member of the Westchester County Board of Realtors, operating as Jasper Real Estate, in South Salem, New York. Margaret Jasper maintains a website at http://www.JasperLawOffice.com.

Ms. Jasper is the author and general editor of the following legal almanacs: AIDS Law; The Americans with Disabilities Act; Animal Rights Law; The Law of Attachment and Garnishment; Bankruptcy Law for the Individual Debtor; Individual Bankruptcy and Restructuring; Banks and their Customers; The Law of Buying and Selling; The Law of Capital Punishment; The Law of Child Custody; Commercial Law; Consumer Rights Law; The Law of Contracts; Copyright Law; Credit Cards and the Law; The Law of Debt Collection; Dictionary of Selected Legal Terms; The Law of Dispute Resolution; The Law of Drunk Driving; Education Law; Elder Law; Employee Rights in the Workplace; Employment Discrimination Under Title VII; Environmental Law; Estate Planning; Everyday Legal Forms; Harassment in the Workplace; Health Care and Your Rights. Home Mortgage Law Primer; Hospital Liability Law; Identity Theft and How To Protect Yourself; Insurance Law; International Adoption; The Law of Immigration; Juvenile Justice and Children's Law; Labor Law; Landlord-Tenant Law; The Law of

Libel and Slander; Marriage and Divorce; The Law of Medical Malpractice; Motor Vehicle Law; The Law of No-Fault Insurance; The Law of Obscenity and Pornography; Patent Law; The Law of Personal Injury; Probate Law; The Law of Product Liability; Real Estate Law for the Homeowner and Broker; Religion and the Law; The Right to Die; Law for the Small Business Owner; Social Security Law; Special Education Law; The Law of Speech and the First Amendment; Trademark Law; Victim's Rights Law; The Law of Violence Against Women; Welfare: Your Rights and the Law; and Workers' Compensation Law.

INTRODUCTION

The Internet is a significant source of both commercial and financial activity, and has become this nation's primary medium for the exchange of news, mail, and general information. Unfortunately, these great benefits expose Internet users to serious privacy risks, which can lead to catastrophic results. Thus, it is crucial that Internet users understand how to safely and securely "surf the net," without exposing themselves to all sorts of criminal activity and other intrusions into their personal information.

This almanac discusses some of the most important security methods, including the effective use of passwords, utilizing virus software, installing firewalls, understanding encyrption technology, and being vigilant about the type of information one shares on the Internet. An overview of the problem of Internet identity theft is also presented.

The legal obligations of various entities, particularly financial institutions, in protecting the private information of Internet users is also explored, including Internet privacy policies and applicable laws. A discussion of online privacy protection for children, including the governing law, is also discussed.

In addition, this almanac sets forth the role of the Federal Trade Commission (FTC) in enforcing privacy rights, including a review of some of the major enforcement cases brought by the FTC.

The Appendix provides resource directories, applicable statutes, and other pertinent information and data. The Glossary contains definitions of many of the terms used throughout the almanac.

CHAPTER 1:
AN OVERVIEW OF PRIVACY AND THE INTERNET

IN GENERAL

The "Internet" was initially conceived for military purposes in 1962 as a decentralized computer network to protect the ability of the military command to communicate in case of a nuclear attack. It took seven years to develop the prototype, which initially consisted of four computer networks located at three universities and one research facility.

Since that time, the Internet has grown tremendously. It has provided the public with a revolutionary tool for marketing, banking and communication. We are able to access all sorts of information and entertainment; perform banking and other financial activities online; purchase products from all over the world; and even work conveniently from home or away while still being able to communicate efficiently with our main office location.

Unfortunately, along with the tremendous advantages the Internet provides, there are great risks. Internet use opens up a gateway to our personal information, our security and safety. The Internet enhances the availability and accessibility of personal identifying information, and thus creates greater risks for consumers and greater opportunities for criminal activity.

Registering for online services generally requires the consumer to provide personal information, including financial information. In addition, there are many scams being perpetrated on the Internet which fool the consumer into revealing personal information. Those seeking to invade the privacy of Internet users, often for criminal purposes, are constantly seeking to decode the massive amount of data being transmitted on the Internet.

Therefore, it is crucial that Internet users carefully safeguard their personal information to protect their privacy and minimize the risk of becoming a victim. As further discussed in this almanac, securing a computer and protecting one's personal information is largely a matter of routine maintenance. Nevertheless, these procedures are frequently neglected by the average Internet user, exposing them to a potential disaster.

DEMOGRAPHICS

According to the Federal Trade Commission (FTC), there are approximately 177 million Internet users in the United States, and 500 million world-wide. In the United States, children and young adults make up the greatest number of people who use the Internet. According to a study conducted in 2000 by the Ipsos Reid Group, 85 percent of Americans aged 12-24 used the Internet regularly, compared to 59 percent of the rest of the adult population.

THE PRIVACY THREAT

When an individual signs on to the Internet, e.g., through America Online or another Internet Service Provider (ISP), they engage in "online communication." The information that they communicate necessarily passes through multiple computer systems to reach its destination. As the information passes through the various computer systems, the capability of the computer system to "capture" and "store" the information exists.

There is no way that anyone using the Internet can be guaranteed complete privacy of the information transmitted online. Nevertheless, as discussed below, the degree to which one's personal information is potentially exposed depends, in large part, on the nature of their online activity.

Broadband Internet Access

Broadband Internet access has become available through cable, satellite and telephone companies. Broadband service keeps the consumer connected to the Internet whenever their computer is turned on as opposed to signing on and off each time they want to go online.

The problem with broadband Internet access is that it makes the consumer more vulnerable to having their private information accessed. Consider installing a "firewall," i.e., special software that provides a barrier and controls access to a computer by unauthorized users.

If you're concerned about others accessing your computer files when you have temporarily stepped away from the computer, but you don't want to keep turning the computer on and off, you can password protect your PC screen saver so that only you can deactivate it.

Hackers

Hackers are able to access home computers through an open Internet connection giving them access to the user's private information. To minimize the risk, it is important to log off the Internet after each session—especially if you have broadband internet access. Any computer connected to the Internet is a potential target for malicious hackers.

Public Forums

If you participate in a public activity, such as a public forum or newsgroup, the information posted is open to the public. Messages and comments can generally be viewed by anyone with Internet access, and those postings often include the user's screen name, e-mail address and Internet service provider.

Further, one may think that, by entering a "chat room," their online conversation is private. However, any individual in that chat room can copy the content of any other individual's online conversation and disseminate it at will over the Internet. This is so even if entry to the forum or chat room is restricted to members with passwords.

In addition, if a user posts a message in an online newsletter or listserve—an online mailing list that allows individuals or organizations to send e-mail to groups of people at one time—their message will be read by all members of the group. If the user wants to reply privately, they must send the message to that individual's specific e-mail address, and not the address of the newsletter or listserve.

Internet Service Providers

A subscriber's ISP often downloads graphics and program upgrades to the subscriber's computer, however, a message is usually sent to the subscriber alerting them to the download of such information. Nevertheless, certain service providers have admitted to inadvertently, and sometimes intentionally, accessing information from the subscriber's computer without their knowledge or consent, purportedly to enhance customer service.

In addition, most ISPs publish online member directories which may contain a subscriber's personal information. Some ISPs sell their member lists to marketing services. An ISP will generally remove a subscriber's name and information from their list upon request.

E-Mail Systems

Most ISPs do offer some mechanism by which a subscriber can send a personal, private message to another, e.g. via e-mail, and viewing or disclosing such messages are generally protected under the Electronic Communications Privacy Act (ECPA). However, there are a number of exceptions to this provision.

For example, the ISP is permitted to view private e-mails if they believe the sender intends to damage the computer system or harm another user. In addition, the ISP is permitted to view and disclose private e-mails if either the sender or recipient of the message consents, and such consent may have automatically been given in the initial agreement between the subscriber and the ISP.

Selected provisions of the Electronic Communications Privacy Act are set forth at Appendix 1 of this almanac.

In addition, certain "enhanced" e-mail messages may contain a graphic called a "web bug," which enables a third party to monitor who is reading the message, confirm when it is read, and record the IP address of the viewer, a multi-digit number that uniquely identifies the viewer's computer. There are software programs available that can detect web bugs.

Cookies

Many websites deposit data about a user's visit to the site—e.g., their name, address, and preferences—on the hard drive of the user's computer, so that they can identify the user when he or she returns to visit the site without the user having to reenter the information. The website might also offer products tailored to the user's interests, based on the recorded preferences. The data is stored in the form of small text files known as "cookies."

Although most cookies are used only by the website that placed the data on the user's computer, some cookies—called third-party cookies—may transmit the user's data to an advertising clearinghouse which may in turn share that data with other online marketers.

Recording an Internet user's preferences and browsing patterns is a valuable marketing device used by website hosts. They use the information to target potential customers and create "mailing lists." This can result in numerous unsolicited e-mails, generally referred to as "spam."

Internet users who prefer not to have cookies stored on their hard drive can delete the data using their web browser or certain software products designed to detect cookies. Information on detecting and deleting cookies is further set forth in Chapter 4 of this almanac.

Domain Registration Services

Many Internet users obtain their own website name, known as a "domain name." Domain registrations are public information and anyone can look up the owner of a domain name online by using certain online services. Therefore, it is important not to use personal information when registering for a domain name.

Employer Access

Employers who operate e-mail systems are allowed to monitor the content of employee e-mails on their system. Therefore, employees have no expectation of privacy in the e-mails they send from an employer-owned e-mail system. This is so even if the e-mail is sent from the employee's home, because a copy is still stored on the employer's main computer server.

Those who use e-mail systems at work are advised to obtain a separate account for their personal e-mail. This would allow the user to check their personal messages without using the workplace e-mail server. Some private accounts can be configured to enable the user to check their personal mail from work without downloading it onto their company's computer.

Law Enforcement Access

Congress enacted the Privacy Protection Act of 1980 (PPA) to prohibit the unrestricted search and seizure of materials possessed by publishers. Under the PPA, government officials or employees are prohibited from searching or seizing any work product or documentary materials held by "a person reasonably believed to have a purpose to disseminate to the public a newspaper, book, broadcast, or other similar form of public communication," unless there is probable cause to believe that the person possessing the material has committed or is committing the criminal offense to which the materials relate; or there is reason to believe that the immediate seizure of the material is necessary to prevent the death of, or serious bodily injury to, a human being.

Thus, law enforcement officials are required to use subpoenas to obtain evidence from persons engaged in First Amendment activities. Arguably, the PPA extends protection to online activities, such as e-mail, bulletin boards, chat rooms, etc., pursuant to the "other form of public communication" clause of the Act.

The Privacy Protection Act of 1980 is set forth at Appendix 2 of this almanac.

ISPs must honor court orders or subpoenas which request disclosure of the private information of their subscribers. However, since the terrorist attacks of September 11th, law enforcement access to online activities has been greatly expanded pursuant to the U.S. Patriot Act, which was subsequently passed by Congress in November 2001. For example, law enforcement is now entitled to certain records concerning online activity which would have previously required a court order.

Selected provisions of the U.S. Patriot Act are set forth at Appendix 3 of this almanac.

PRIVACY LAWS

Numerous privacy laws have been enacted by federal and state governments, in large part due to computer technology and the changes in information gathering that have occurred over the past twenty years. The laws vary, but their common goal is to protect individuals from the unauthorized use of the collected information and government access to private records.

A summary of federal, state and local privacy laws is set forth at Appendix 4 of this almanac.

In addition, there are many organizations dedicated to assisting the Internet user in maintaining the privacy of their personal information. These organizations offer advice and guidance on Internet usage and privacy issues, and many are advocates who lobby the government for more stringent privacy legislation. Their websites provide a host of information on the practical and legal issues concerning privacy on the Internet.

An Internet privacy resource directory is set forth at Appendix 5 of this almanac.

PRIVACY POLICIES

Companies operating online often ask their customers personal information so that they can gather marketing information concerning the people who visit their website. The information gathered may also be shared with others for marketing and other purposes. Privacy policies vary among websites, therefore, the consumer is advised to read them carefully.

It is important to determine whether the website you visit has a privacy policy. If so, the privacy policy should detail the following:

1. The type of information collected;

2. How the information is used;

3. Whether the information is shared with third parties; and

4. What control the consumer has over their personal information.

Privacy policies also should tell the consumer how they can find out what information has been collected by the website so that erroneous information can be corrected or deleted. The privacy policy should also explain how the company restricts their employees' access to the consumer's personal information.

Consumers may also have the choice to "opt out" of having their information used in various ways. If there is such an "opt out" policy, the consumer must generally affirmatively state that they do not want their information used. Otherwise, the information will be disseminated. meaning that it will be used unless you say "no." If there is an "opt in" policy, this means that the consumer's personal information cannot be used unless they affirmatively state that they want their information used.

Many websites also ask the consumer's permission to contact them in the future by e-mail with notices, updates, offers and other information. The consumer should have the option of declining permission for future contact.

Privacy policies are discussed more fully in Chapter 5 of this almanac.

CHAPTER 2:
THE ROLE OF THE FEDERAL TRADE COMMISSION

IN GENERAL

The Federal Trade Commission (FTC) is the nation's primary consumer protection organization. Privacy is the central element of the Federal Trade Commission's (FTC) mission to protect the public. Since the expansion of the Internet, the need to educate consumers and businesses about the importance of personal information privacy, including the security of personal information, has become an utmost priority for the FTC. The FTC also actively investigates privacy violations and aggressively enforces the nation's privacy laws. The FTC has also developed a number of privacy initiatives, as discussed below.

Anti-Spam Enforcement Initiative

As further discussed in this almanac, junk e-mail, known as spam, presents serious safety concerns for consumers as well as a tremendous burden on the Internet. Spam e-mail often contains deceptive and fraudulent schemes, such as chain letters, pyramid schemes and other types of scams intended to victimize unsophisticated Internet users. The FTC is increasing its enforcement activities against these illegal activities.

Identity Theft Prevention

Identity theft is a swiftly growing national problem due, in large part, to the ability of identity thieves to access an individual's personal identifying information through the Internet. As further discussed in this almanac, identity theft can ruin a consumer's credit and make it difficult, if not impossible, for the victim to get a loan, rent an apartment or even get a job.

Congress has appointed the FTC as the nation's central repository for identity theft complaints. The FTC has received more than 100,000 consumers complaints concerning identity theft. The FTC collects data on identity theft and uses it to identify patterns to assist law enforcement agencies in prosecuting identity thieves.

Anti-Pretexting Initiative

"Pretexting" is the practice of fraudulently obtaining an individual's personal financial information, such as account numbers and balances, by contacting financial institutions under the pretext of being a customer. Pretexting is prohibited by the Gramm-Leach-Bliley Act. The FTC actively investigates this practice, seeks injunctions against offenders, and aggressively enforces the law.

Accuracy in Credit Reporting Initiative

The FTC works to make sure that all participants in the credit reporting system meet their obligations regarding the accuracy of a consumer's credit information. The FTC also requires that consumers are notified when information in a credit report is the reason for a denial of credit, insurance or employment.

Enforcement of Privacy Promises

Companies with whom consumers do business make privacy promises to their customers. The FTC has encouraged websites to post privacy notices and honor the promises made and, as a result, many websites now post their privacy policies online. The FTC also brings enforcement actions against companies who fail to honor the promises found in their privacy statements.

Children's Online Privacy Initiative

As further discussed in this almanac, The Children's Online Privacy Protection Act of 1998 prevents the collection of personally identifiable information from children without their parent's consent. The FTC enforces the provisions of COPPA, and provides educational materials to parents concerning their children's online activities.

Privacy Complaints Hotline

The FTC operates a toll-free hotline number (1-877-FTC-HELP) as well as a complaint form on its website (www.ftc.gov) for consumers to report privacy-related complaints, as well as fraudulent and deceptive business practices. The FTC enters Internet, telemarketing, identity theft and other fraud-related complaints into Consumer Sentinel, a secure, online database available to hundreds of civil and criminal law enforcement agencies in the U.S. and overseas.

The Gramm-Leach-Bliley Act (GLBA)

As further discussed in Chapter 6 of this almanac, the Gramm-Leach-Bliley Act (the "Safeguards Rule"), signed into law in 1999, requires financial institutions to provide privacy notices to consumers, and allows consumers, with certain exceptions, to choose whether their financial institutions may share their information with third parties. The FTC has undertaken enforcement efforts to ensure that financial institutions comply with the law and has implemented an outreach program to increase consumer awareness of the notices.

Public Workshops

The FTC continues to explore the privacy implications of new and emerging technologies through workshops, reports and other public meetings. The FTC also monitors the development of the Platform for Privacy Preferences, an important technology that will enable consumers to specify their privacy preferences electronically and screen out sites that do not meet them.

ENFORCEMENT ACTIONS

The FTC guards against unfairness and deception by enforcing companies' privacy promises about how they collect, use and secure a consumer's personal information, pursuant to Section 5 of the FTC Act. The FTC has brought a number of cases to enforce the promises in privacy statements, including promises about the security of consumers' personal information.

Some of the FTC's most noteworthy privacy enforcement actions are set forth below.

The Microsoft Case

Microsoft Corporation, a provider of software, services, and Internet technologies for personal and business computing, operates three related Internet services: Passport Single Sign-In, known as "Passport," Passport Express Purchase, known as "Passport Wallet," and Kids Passport.

Passport collects personal information from consumers and allows them to sign in at any participating website with a single name and password. Passport Wallet collects and stores consumers' credit card numbers, and billing and shipping addresses, and enables consumers to use the stored information when making purchases at participating websites. Kids Passport allows parents to create Passport accounts for their children that can limit the collection of personal information by participating websites.

Microsoft's Passport privacy policies included statements such as, "Passport achieves a high level of Web Security by using technologies and systems designed to prevent unauthorized access to your personal information," and "Your Passport is protected by powerful online security and a strict privacy policy."

The Kids Passport privacy policy included statements such as, "Microsoft Kids Passport allows parents to consent to the collection, use and sharing of their children's information with Passport participating sites. . . . You can choose to allow Passport to share all of the information in your child's Passport profile with a participating site or service, or you can limit the information shared to just a unique identifier or age range. . . ."

The FTC initiated its investigation of the Passport services following a July 2001 complaint from a coalition of consumer groups led by the Electronic Privacy Information Center (EPIC).

According to the Commission's complaint, Microsoft falsely represented that:

1. It employs reasonable and appropriate measures under the circumstances to maintain and protect the privacy and confidentiality of consumers' personal information collected through its Passport and Passport Wallet services, including credit card numbers and billing information stored in Passport Wallet;

2. Purchases made with Passport Wallet are generally safer or more secure than purchases made at the same site without Passport Wallet when, in fact, most consumers received identical security at those sites regardless of whether they used Passport Wallet to complete their transactions;

3. Passport did not collect any personally identifiable information other than that described in its privacy policy when, in fact, Passport collected and held, for a limited time, a personally identifiable sign-in history for each user; and

4. The Kids Passport program provided parents control over what information participating Web sites could collect from their children.

A copy of the Microsoft Complaint is set forth at Appendix 6 of this almanac.

As a result of the FTC's enforcement efforts, Microsoft Corporation agreed to settle the FTC charges regarding the privacy and security of personal information collected from consumers through its "Passport" web services. As part of the settlement, the FTC entered into a consent order with Microsoft which prohibits any misrepresentation of information practices in connection with Passport and other similar services. It also requires

Microsoft to implement and maintain a comprehensive information security program for Passport and similar services. In addition, Microsoft must have its security program certified as meeting or exceeding the standards in the consent order by an independent professional every two years.

A copy of the Microsoft Consent Order is set forth at Appendix 7 of this almanac.

Liberty Financial Companies, Inc.—Young Investor Website

In an effort to address children's online privacy, the FTC brought an enforcement action against Liberty Financial Companies, Inc., the operator of the Young Investor website. Liberty Financial is a large asset management company based in Boston, Massachusetts. It provides various fixed and variable annuities as well as management of private and institutional accounts in addition to mutual funds. The Young Investor website is directed to children and teens, and focuses on issues relating to money and investing.

The FTC alleged that the website featured several different areas that appealed to children by, for example, using contests and prizes. According to the FTC, at one such area, the Measure Up Survey area, children were invited to provide financial information including the amount of the child's weekly allowance; types of financial gifts received; spending habits; part time work history; plans for college; and family finances.

In addition, the site asked for personal identifying information such as name, address, age and e-mail address in connection with providing the children with an e-mail newsletter and eligibility to receive prizes. At the beginning of the survey, Liberty Financial expressly stated that, "All of your answers will be totally anonymous."

According to the FTC's complaint, the personal information about the child and the family's finances was maintained in an identifiable manner because Liberty Financial could identify individuals with their responses to the survey. In addition, the Commission's complaint alleges that Liberty Financial did not send participants the company's Young Investor e-mail newsletter as promised. Finally, the complaint alleges that the website falsely represented that every three months, a participant who submitted the personal information would be selected to win his or her choice of certain prizes.

A copy of the Liberty Financial Complaint is set forth at Appendix 8 of this almanac.

As a result of the FTC's enforcement efforts, the FTC entered into a consent order with Liberty Financial which prohibits Liberty Financial from making any false statements about the collection or use of personal information from children under the age of eighteen.

The consent order defines "personal information" as "individually identifiable information about an individual collected online" such as first and last name, home or other physical address including street name and name of a city or town, e-mail address, telephone number, social security number or any information concerning the child or the parents of that child that the website collects online from the child and combines with an identifier described above.

In addition, for children under 13, the consent order prohibits Liberty Financial from collecting personal information if Liberty Financial has actual knowledge that the child does not have a parent's permission to provide the information. Liberty Financial must also post a clear and prominent privacy statement on its websites directed to children under 13 explaining Liberty Financial's practices with regard to its collection and use of personal information. The notice must disclose what information is collected, its intended uses, to whom it will be disclosed, and the means by which a parent can access and remove the information that has been collected.

The order also requires Liberty Financial to obtain "verifiable parental consent" before collecting and using personal identifying information from children under 13. These requirements are consistent with the requirements of the Children's Online Privacy Protection Act of 1998, and the consent order expressly provides that compliance with that statute, and its implementing regulations, will be deemed compliance with the order.

A copy of the Liberty Financial Consent Order is set forth at Appendix 9 of this almanac.

Eli Lilly and Company

Eli Lilly and Company, a pharmaceutical company based in Indiana, manufactures, markets, and sells several drugs, including the anti-depressant medication Prozac. Lilly also operates the Prozac.com website, which the company promotes as "Your Guide to Evaluating and Recovering from Depression." Several of Lilly's websites, including www.prozac.com and www.lilly.com, collect personal information from visitors.

From March 15, 2000 until June 22, 2001, Lilly offered consumers the "Medi-messenger" e-mail reminder service. Consumers who used Medi-messenger could design and receive personal e-mail messages to remind them to take or refill their medication. Once a consumer registered for Medi-messenger, the reminder messages were automatically e-mailed from Lilly to the subscriber at the e-mail address provided, and according to the subscriber's requested schedule. These reminders were individualized e-mails and did not identify any other subscribers to the service.

On June 27, 2001, a Lilly employee created a new computer program to access Medi-messenger subscribers' e-mail addresses and sent them an e-mail message announcing the termination of the Medi-messenger service. The June 27th e-mail message included all of the recipients' e-mail addresses within the "To:" line of the message, thereby unintentionally disclosing to each individual subscriber the e-mail addresses of all 669 Medi-messenger subscribers.

According to the FTC's complaint, Lilly claimed that it employs measures and takes steps appropriate under the circumstances to maintain and protect the privacy and confidentiality of personal information obtained from or about consumers through its Prozac.com and Lilly.com websites. For example, Lilly's privacy policies included statements such as, "Eli Lilly and Company respects the privacy of visitors to its websites, and we feel it is important to maintain our guests' privacy as they take advantage of this resource."

The FTC complaint also alleges that Lilly's claim of privacy and confidentiality was deceptive because Lilly failed to maintain or implement internal measures appropriate under the circumstances to protect sensitive consumer information, which led to the company's unintentional June 27th disclosure of Medi-messenger subscribers' personal information. In fact, according to the complaint, Lilly failed to:

(i) provide appropriate training for its employees regarding consumer privacy and information security;

(ii) provide appropriate oversight and assistance for the employee who sent out the e-mail, who had no prior experience in creating, testing, or implementing the computer program used; and

(iii) implement appropriate checks and controls on the process, such as reviewing the computer program with experienced personnel and pretesting the program internally before sending out the e-mail.

In addition, Lilly's failure to implement appropriate measures also violated a number of its own written security procedures.

A copy of the Eli Lilly Complaint is set forth at Appendix 10 of this almanac.

As a result of the FTC's enforcement efforts, Lilly agreed to settle FTC charges regarding the unauthorized disclosure of sensitive personal information collected from consumers through its Prozac.com website. As part of the settlement, the FTC entered into a consent order with Lilly under which Lilly was required to take appropriate security measures to protect consumers' privacy. The consent order also bars misrepresentations about the extent to which Lilly maintains and protects the privacy or confidentiality of any personal information collected from or about consumers.

Additionally, Lilly was required to establish and maintain a four-stage information security program designed to establish and maintain reasonable and appropriate administrative, technical, and physical safeguards to protect consumers' personal information against any reasonably anticipated threats or hazards to its security, confidentiality, or integrity, and to protect such information against unauthorized access, use, or disclosure.

A copy of the Eli Lilly Consent Order is set forth at Appendix 11 of this almanac.

Toysmart.com

Toysmart.com was a popular website that marketed and sold educational and non-violent children's toys over the Internet. Through its website, Toysmart collected detailed personal information about its visitors, including name, address, billing information, shopping preferences, and family profiles—which included the names and birthdates of children.

Since September 1999, Toysmart had posted a privacy policy which stated that information collected from customers will never be shared with third parties. However, when it subsequently ran into financial difficulties, it attempted to sell all of its assets, including its detailed customer databases.

On July 10, 2000, the FTC filed a lawsuit in the U.S. District Court for the District of Massachusetts against Toysmart to prevent the sale of the customer information. The FTC subsequently amended its complaint against Toysmart alleging that Toysmart also collected personal information from children under 13 without notifying parents or obtaining parental consent, in violation of the Children's Online Privacy Protection Act of 1998. COPPA requires that operators of commercial websites and online services directed to children under 13, and general audience sites that know that they are collecting personal information from children, obtain parental consent before personal information is collected from their children.

A copy of the Toysmart Amended Complaint is set forth at Appendix 12 of this almanac.

As a result of the FTC's enforcement efforts, Toysmart agreed to settle FTC charges that the company violated Section 5 of the FTC Act by misrepresenting to consumers that personal information would never be shared with third parties and then disclosing, selling, or offering that information for sale in violation of the company's own privacy statement. The consent order forbids the sale of this customer information except under very limited circumstances.

Pursuant to the consent order, Toysmart was required to file an order in Bankruptcy Court prohibiting Toysmart from selling the customer list as a stand-alone asset. The consent order only allowed a sale of such lists as a package which included the entire website, and only to a "Qualified Buyer"—an entity that is in a related market and that expressly agrees to be Toysmart's successor-in-interest as to the customer information.

Further, in the event that the Bankruptcy Court does not approve the sale of the customer information to a Qualified Buyer, Toysmart was ordered to delete or destroy all customer information. In the interim, Toysmart was obligated to abide by its privacy statement.

A copy of the Toysmart Consent Order is set forth at Appendix 13 of this almanac.

CHAPTER 3:
E-MAIL

IN GENERAL

Internet users communicate with each other online using e-mail and instant messages. It is an immediate way of transmitting information to others, and has become very popular as a means of communication in both personal and business affairs. Unfortunately, as set forth below, communicating online does not afford the same level of privacy that written correspondence offers.

SECURING E-MAIL

E-mail is a way of communicating electronically from one computer to another computer. All kinds of information can be sent via e-mail, including text messages, letters, documents, pictures, etc.

Encryption

E-mail is generally not secure and can be intercepted and read by others. Therefore, it would be unwise to transmit any personal identifying or financial information in an e-mail unless you use e-mail cryptography software to scramble your messages in code. Encryption is a method of scrambling an e-mail message or file so that it is gibberish to anyone who does not know how to unscramble it.

The privacy advantage of encryption is that anything encrypted is virtually inaccessible to anyone other than the designated recipient. Thus, private information may be encrypted and then transmitted, stored, or distributed without fear that it will be read by others.

Anonymous Remailers

Anonymous remailers were created to address privacy risks and concerns by allowing the user to send anonymous e-mail messages. An anonymous remailer is a special e-mail server that acts as a middleman and strips outgoing e-mail of all personally identifying information, then forwards it to its destination, usually with the IP address of the remailer attached.

Deleting Stored E-Mail

Every time an e-mail message is sent, a number of copies of that e-mail message are created. One copy is stored locally on the sender's computer, another on the sender's ISP's system, another on the recipient's computer, and one copy is stored on the recipient's ISP's system.

You can also delete the stored copy of your e-mail by opening the "sent mail" folder in the e-mail program and delete the e-mail by removing it to the trash folder, and then emptying the trash folder.

Web-Based E-Mail Service

Another way of keeping e-mail private when you share a computer is to use a web-based e-mail service. Web-based e-mail services store the user's e-mail on a computer server, such as a web page, instead of the user's computer. Again, make sure you keep your password private.

Employer Access

As set forth in Chapter 1, employers are legally allowed to view and monitor any e-mails on the employer's e-mail system, even if the e-mail is sent from the employee's home. Therefore, employees who use the employer's e-mail system are advised to obtain a separate account for their personal e-mail, which would allow the user to check their personal messages without using the workplace e-mail server.

Forwarding

Recipients of an e-mail can forward that e-mail to an unlimited number of additional recipients with the simple click of the mouse. The sender has no control over how many people ultimately view the e-mail he or she sends. If you don't want the e-mail you send to be viewed by an unlimited number of people, you must send it to someone who you can trust will not forward it without your consent.

VERIFICATION

The nature of e-mail makes it difficult to verify that the person who signs the e-mail is the actual person who is sending the e-mail. With regular mail, you can generally identify the sender by their handwriting, the signature, or the letterhead on which the correspondence is sent. However, you cannot identify an individual from the font type they use to create the e-mail. Thus, it is possible to unwittingly correspond with a complete stranger who is pretending to be someone known to the user. Nevertheless, there is software available on the market that can assist senders and recipients of e-mails with the identification process, such as the digital signature.

VIRUSES

From time to time, the media reports on "viruses" that are circulating in cyberspace, such as the infamous "Melissa" virus. A virus can do considerable damage to computer programs and files and can also reveal personal information stored on the computer.

To protect yourself from accidentally downloading a virus to your computer, do not open any e-mail attachments from unknown senders. Even if you are familiar with the sender, if the subject matter appears suspicious, do not open it. Those who circulate these viruses are able to access a computer user's mailing list and e-mail the virus so that it appears to be coming from a known sender.

Also be aware that certain programs available for download on the Internet may contain viruses. Check out the particular download carefully before accessing it. It is advisable to install and regularly update anti-virus software on your computer which will search for viruses and alert you to their presence.

SPAM

Most Internet users are bombarded with numerous unsolicited junk e-mail messages from businesses and individuals seeking to market their products, services and scams over the Internet. These e-mails are known as "spam." A business or individual will generally buy a list of e-mail addresses from a third party, and then use software that allows them to send messages to everyone on the list within seconds. The "harvesting of e-mail addresses is generally automated. Spam e-mail finds its way to new e-mail addresses soon after they are used publicly for the first time.

Statistics

The FTC conducted an Internet study using undercover e-mail addresses in order to find out which areas of the Internet received the most spam e-mail. According to the FTC study:

86 percent of the addresses posted to web pages received spam. It didn't matter where the addresses were posted on the page. If the address had the "@" sign in it, it drew spam.

1. 86 percent of the addresses posted to newsgroups received spam.

2. Chat rooms are virtual magnets for spam. One address posted in a chat room received spam nine minutes after it first was used.

3. 50 percent of the addresses posted on free personal web page services received spam,

4. 27 percent of addresses posted to message boards received spam e-mail.

5. 9 percent of addresses listed in e-mail service directories received spam e-mail.

6. 9 percent of addresses posted in instant message service user profiles received spam e-mail.

FTC investigators found that e-mail addresses posted in other areas on the Internet received less spam e-mail. "Whois" domain name registries, online resume services, and online dating services did not receive any spam during the six weeks investigation.

The investigators also found that the spam received was not related to the address used thus consumers with e-mail addresses received a variety of types of spam e-mail. For example, some e-mail addresses posted to children's newsgroups received a large amount of spam promoting adult web sites and advertising hallucinogenic drugs.

Spam Reduction Methods

As set forth below, there are a number of methods designed to reduce the amount of unsolicited e-mail messages.

Do Not Publicize Your E-Mail Address

Since the individuals who compile the lists of e-mail addresses harvest those addresses from the Internet, you should try not to display their e-mail address publicly over the Internet. You should also request that your Internet service provider remove your name from membership directories that are posted on the Internet. In addition, you should try not to publish your e-mail address in chat rooms and on websites.

Mask Your E-Mail Address

Masking involves putting a word or phrase in your e-mail address so that it will generally trick a harvesting computer program, but not a person. For example, if your e-mail address is "johndoe@myisp.com," you could mask it as "johndoe@spamaway.myisp.com."

However, some newsgroup services or message boards won't allow you to mask your e-mail address and some harvesting programs may be able to pick out common masks.

Use Two E-Mail Addresses

Many websites require the user to provide their e-mail address before they can sign up for online services or purchase products online. In that case, it might be prudent to use two e-mail addresses and designate one for personal use and one for public use on the Internet. If you use chat rooms, use a screen name that's not associated with your e-mail address. Consider using the screen name only for online chat.

Use Disposable E-Mail Addresses

There are services that provide Internet users with "disposable" e-mail addresses that forward e-mail to the permanent e-mail account. Then, if one of the disposable addresses begins to receive spam e-mail, the user can turn it off without affecting their permanent address.

Create a Unique E-Mail Address

Another method of trying to avoid being spammed is to create a unique e-mail address. Your choice of e-mail address may affect the amount of spam you receive. Some spammers use "dictionary attacks" to e-mail many possible name combinations at large ISPs or e-mail services, trying to come up with common names and variations to locate valid e-mail addresses in order to compile a list.

For example, marysmith@aol.com and variations of this e-mail address are very easy for a spammer to validate. It is much more difficult to try and decode an e-mail address that is randomly made up of numbers and letters.

Filter Junk E-Mail

Many e-mail systems have screening capabilities which allow the user to limit the amount of unsolicited commercial e-mail that ends up in the user's inbox. Junk mail filters use certain criteria to filter out junk mail. For example, junk mail filters identify items such as font style, symbols, and phrasing to classify messages as junk mail.

The junk mail is then diverted to another folder, according to the user's preferences. Junk mail may be sent directly to the trash, or to a bulk e-mail folder, where it generally remains for a certain amount of time before being automatically deleted. The user can view the contents of the folder at any time to make sure the junk mail filter is not eliminating e-mails that the user may want to receive.

Check Out Website Privacy Policies

In addition, it is important to check the privacy policy for any website you visit and find out whether the company sells or shares its visitors' identifying information before submitting your personal information. If the privacy policy indicates that the company does compile such information, it is best not to visit that website or you risk opening yourself up to more unsolicited commercial e-mail. Some websites allow the user to "opt out" of receiving e-mail from third parties if the user so chooses.

E-Mail Preference Service

Another way of reducing the amount of unsolicited commercial e-mail is to register up for the e-Mail Preference Service (e-MPS) offered by the Direct Marketing Association (www.e-mps.org). All DMA members who wish to send unsolicited commercial e-mail must delete from their e-mail prospecting lists the names of any individuals who have registered their e-mail address with e-MPS. The service is also available to non-DMA members.

COMMON E-MAIL SCAMS

Many consumers have lost thousands of dollars to these types of deceptive schemes. According to the FTC, many unsolicited e-mail messages contain false information about the sender and/or misleading subject lines, and extravagant earnings or performance claims about goods and services. This widespread ability to disseminate false and misleading claims is the FTC's main concern with spam e-mail. Some common deceptive spam e-mail scams which an Internet user may encounter include illegal chain letters; work-at-home schemes; weight loss programs; credit repair offers; and advance-fee loan offers.

Nigerian Advance-Fee Fraud

According to the FTC, the Nigerian advance-fee fraud scheme has reached epidemic proportions, with some Internet users reportedly receiving dozens of these fraudulent offers each day. The e-mails are purportedly sent from Nigerians officials or businessmen who promise financial rewards for assistance in moving large sums of money out of their country. Those who respond to the offer may receive documents which appear official and are asked to provide bank account numbers and a fee to cover costs. After getting as much money out of the victim as possible, the con artists disappear.

Chain E-Mails

Chain letters used to be sent by regular mail, however, since the inception of the Internet, they are now being circulated via "chain e-mails." Chain e-mails generally include a list of names and addresses with instructions to send money to one or more names on a list. The recipient is then instructed to remove one or more names from the list, add their name to the bottom of the list, and e-mail the letter to a certain number of other people with directions on how to "continue the chain" in order for the recipient to receive his or her share of the money. The sender may also state that the chain e-mails are legal.

According to the FTC, chain e-mails are not legal and those who start, send or forward chain e-mail messages are breaking the law and can be prosecuted for mail fraud. Recipients of chain e-mails are advised to file a complaint with their internet service provider and report the offer to the FTC, or to their State Consumer Protection Office.

A directory of State Consumer Protection Offices is set forth at Appendix 14 of this almanac.

Internet Service Provider Scam

According to the FTC, another common scam designed to obtain personal financial information from the consumer involves e-mail requests purportedly sent from the consumer's Internet service provider (ISP). The e-mail request generally advises the consumer that "your account information needs to be updated" or that "the credit card you signed up with is invalid or expired and the information needs to be reentered to keep your account active." Consumers are advised not to respond to any such e-mail request without first checking with their ISP.

FILING A COMPLAINT

The Federal Trade Commission (FTC)

The Federal Trade Commission (FTC) advises Internet users to forward unsolicited or deceptive e-mail messages to their e-mail address designated for this purpose (uce@ftc.gov). The FTC uses the unsolicited e-mails stored in this database to pursue law enforcement actions against those who send deceptive spam e-mail.

In addition, the FTC should also be notified if a consumer's request to remove their address from a mailing list is not honored. The FTC has an online complaint form for this purpose on its website (www.ftc.gov). Each complaint is added to the FTC's Consumer Sentinel database and made available to hundreds of law enforcement and consumer protection agencies.

When making a complaint, it is important to include the full e-mail header of the spam e-mail. The information in the header makes it possible for the FTC to follow up on the complaint.

The User's Internet Service Provider

The user should also send a copy of the unsolicited e-mail to the abuse desk of their own Internet service provider (ISP). Often the e-mail address is abuse@yourispname.com or postmaster@yourispname.com. Include a copy of the spam, along with the full e-mail header, and at the top of the message, state that you're complaining about being spammed. Forwarding your spam to your ISP lets them know about the spam problem on their system and helps them to stop it.

The Sender's Internet Service Provider

A complaint should also be made with the abuse desk of the sender's ISP. Most ISPs want to stop spammers who abuse their system. Include a copy of the message and the full e-mail header information, and state that you're complaining about spam.

INSTANT MESSAGING

Instant messaging is the ability to communicate with another on the internet in a chat-like mode. Generally, the user sets up their instant messaging network so that they are notified when an individual on their list is online. They can then send an instant message to that person, who can respond immediately on screen. It is much like talking on the telephone, except the parties type their messages back and forth.

As a privacy feature, most instant message programs allow users to be invisible to all other users except those selected to appear on their instant messaging list.

CHAPTER 4:
E-COMMERCE

IN GENERAL

According to the Federal Trade Commission (FTC), it is estimated that on-line commercial activity—referred to as "e-commerce"—will exceed $1 trillion dollars in 2003. Consumers are increasingly using the Internet to shop, bank and invest online. This increase in online shopping underscores the need for security and privacy of online transactions. In fact, privacy and security are the two most important reasons some consumers are reluctant to shop online.

SECURING ONLINE TRANSACTIONS

All companies require information about the consumer in order to process a transaction. Although it may be impossible to protect oneself completely from fraud and deception in both online and off-line purchases, there are some steps the consumer can take to make it less likely their personal information will be intercepted, as further discussed below.

ANONYMOUS REMAILERS

Consumers who are reluctant to provide any personal information online may use a program that masks their identity, such as an "anonymous remailer," by enabling the consumer to make their online transactions through third parties.

SECURE BROWSERS

A browser is special software that allows the user to navigate through the internet and view various websites. Most computers come with a browser installed, e.g., Microsoft Internet Explorer and Netscape Navigator. Some browsers are available for downloading on the internet at no cost to the user. Browsers transmit a user's personal information to website operators, including but not limited to the user's ISP, and websites the user has visited.

The consumer should make sure that they use a secure browser when providing personal identifying or financial information online. A secure browser refers to software that encrypts or scrambles the purchase information sent over the Internet. The consumer should be sure that the browser they use has the latest encryption capabilities available and should comply with industry security standards. If the website states that the consumer's personal identifying or financial information does not need to be encrypted, they should not patronize the website.

Emptying the Cache

The "cache" is an area on the computer's hard drive where copies of the websites the user visits are stored so that the browser can access them locally instead of going to the website. This helps to make browsing faster and easier. However, storage of the user's browsing record can jeopardize the user's privacy, particularly if the user shares the computer with others, or uses a public computer, e.g., in a library or internet cafe.

The browsing record can be deleted by taking the following steps:

1. Click on "edit" in the browser.
2. Scroll down to "preferences."
3. Click on the "empty cache" button.
4. Close the browser.

Cookies

"Cookies" are bits of electronic information in the form of small text files that identify the computer used by a specific customer to a particular website. Cookies are placed on a computer's hard drive when the user visits various websites. Cookies are used by the website to tailor information to the particular customer, such as marketing information, preferences, etc. This data may include the user's name, address, and preferences and browsing patterns.

Cookies inform the website operator that the user has visited the website, and can be used to track the user online and enable the website operator to create a profile of the user without the user's knowledge. If the user has obtained a username and password to access the website, cookies remembers that information so that the user can easily access the website again without having to enter their password each time they visit the site. When the user revisits the same website, it opens the cookie file to access stored information.

Third Party Cookies

Although most cookies are used only by the website that placed the data on the user's computer, some cookies—called third-party cookies—are maintained by websites other than the one the user visited. Third-party cookies may transmit the user's data to an advertising clearinghouse which may in turn share that data with other online marketers. This can lead to many unsolicited commercial e-mails being sent to the user.

Detecting Cookies and Setting Preferences

The presence of cookies on a website can be detected using special software or particular browser settings. You can search the hard drive for a file with the word "cookie" in it—e.g., cookie.txt—to view the cookies that have been stored on your computer. Internet users who prefer not to have cookies stored on their hard drive can set their preferences concerning the cookies that are stored. For example, some users choose to limit third-party cookies. The user can also completely disable the ability for cookies to be placed on their hard drive.

Instructions on how to set "cookies" preferences on the web browser is set forth at Appendix 15 of this almanac.

Newer browsers allow the user to recognize websites that send cookies in advance. The user can then reject the cookies before they are placed on the computer's hard driver rather than having to delete them afterwards.

Javascript

JavaScript is a programming language used to add features to web pages in order to make the website more interactive. Javascript is interpreted by the web browser. Unfortunately, Javascript creates some privacy risks to the user due to "privacy holes" sometimes found in javascript. For example, some "privacy holes" have permitted remote sites to read the URLs from the browser's cache, thus gaining access to the list of websites visited by the user. It is advisable, therefore, to turn Javascript off when visiting unfamiliar websites. In addition, virus detectors can identify whether a specific Javascript has a privacy hole.

PRIVACY STATEMENTS

It is important to review a website's privacy policy to ascertain the security features offered by the site. The user is cautioned not to provide any personal information if they are not satisfied that the website is secure.

Privacy statements are discussed more fully in Chapter 5 of this almanac.

WEBSITE SECURITY

When making a purchase on the Internet, most consumers use credit cards to pay for their online transaction. Before giving out credit card information, it is important to verify the website's online security or encryption capabilities. To determine what type of security system a website uses, the consumer should read the website's privacy statement.

Many websites use Secure Sockets Layer (SSL) technology to encrypt the credit card information that the consumer sends over the Internet. One way of determining whether or not a website is using such technology is to watch the address bar on the screen. At the point where the consumer enters their personal information, such as a credit card number, the prefix on the address should change from "http" to "shttp" or "https."

A different security technology, which works on different principles, is Secure Electronic Transaction (SET) technology, which was developed by MasterCard and Visa. SET assures secure credit and charge card payment using highly encrypted communication between card issuers, merchants and card members. SET also provides an enhanced level of security, confidentiality and transaction integrity. Both SSL and SET technology are designed to make the connection secure.

One can also determine whether a website uses security software if the browser displays the icon of a locked padlock at the bottom of the screen (Netscape Navigator—versions 4.0 and higher); or if there is an icon of an unbroken key at the bottom of the screen (Netscape Navigator—earlier versions); or if there is an icon of a lock on the status bar (Microsoft Internet Explorer).

AVOIDING ONLINE FRAUD

The following precautions should also be taken in order to avoid online fraud and the interception of personal information:

1. Patronize websites of reputable, familiar companies, such as companies who also operate retail stores or mail order catalogues.

2. Patronize companies that display a privacy seal on their website, and read the website's privacy statement to determine their privacy practices.

3. Make sure the company has a physical address and a telephone number so that they can be contacted off-line. A company that lists a post office box instead of a physical address, or one that discloses no contact information, may be a fly-by-night operation set up for illegal purposes.

4. Check with the state Attorney General's Office to see whether there are any adverse reports about the particular company.

5. Give out only the amount of information that is necessary for you to complete the online transaction.

6. When dealing with an unfamiliar company, start out by purchasing a small, inexpensive item to determine how the company handles the order.

7. Use a unique password when registering on a site, randomly combining letters and numbers, and never disclose the password to anyone.

8. Do not send private information by e-mail.

9. Check to make sure you are actually on the official website of the company you want to patronize. Criminals have been known to create websites with names similar to legitimate businesses in order to intercept personal information. One way of checking the legitimacy of a website is to visit http://www.whois.net, a service which sets forth the identity of the registrant of the URL, and the physical address of the company.

10. Often companies hold contests in order to collect names and contact information for future marketing. When deciding whether to enter a contest, consider whether you want the company operating the contest to have access to your personal information.

11. Opt-out of third party information sharing by requesting that a company remove your name from any lists of information that may be shared with third parties.

CHAPTER 5:
PRIVACY STATEMENTS

IN GENERAL

When visiting a website, it is important to check whether the website has a privacy statement, particularly if the website requests the user to enter personal information. A privacy statement describes the way in which the website collects, shares and protects the user's personal information. It is a legally binding document which the website owner must abide by or face legal action.

Internet users should carefully read the privacy policy of all websites with which they do business, including the privacy policy of their own internet service provider. Any website that asks for personal information should have a privacy policy statement. If a website does not post a privacy statement, the user is advised not to patronize that website.

A copy of the American Express Privacy Statement is set forth at Appendix 16 of this almanac.

ELEMENTS OF A PRIVACY STATEMENT

A website's privacy statement should be easily accessible and understandable. Some websites post a simplified version of their privacy policy that is easy for users to read, and provide links to additional information, which may contain more complicated legal or technical information.

A well-drafted privacy policy should provide the user with the following information:

1. The information that is being collected.

2. Whether the information is personally identifiable.

3. The reasons the website collects the information.

4. The appropriateness of the data collection as it relates to the particular activity or transaction.

5. The manner in which the data is collected.

6. Whether the user has a choice regarding the type and quantity of personal information that the site collects.

7. Whether the website uses cookies.

8. Whether the website maintains web logs.

9. How the personal information collected is used by the website.

10. Whether personal information is ever used for a secondary purpose—i.e., a purpose other than that for which the user has provided the information.

11. If personal information is used for a secondary purpose, the user should be so informed.

12. Whether the visitor has consented to secondary use of personal information.

13. Whether the visitor has the option to prohibit secondary use of personal information.

14. Whether the website offers different kinds of service depending on user privacy preferences, e.g., does the website disadvantage users who exercise data collection choices.

15. Whether the user can access the information collected.

16. Whether the user can correct inaccurate data that has been collected.

17. The length of time personal information is stored.

18. The website's complaint procedures.

19. Contact information, such as an e-mail address or phone number, so the user can contact the company if they have any questions about online security or their privacy policy statement.

20. The laws governing data collection.

21. Whether the website collecting the information is regulated by the Privacy Act or any other privacy law.

A sample privacy policy outline is set forth at Appendix 17 of this almanac.

PRIVACY SEALS

Privacy seals are branded symbols of trust on the Internet similar to the Good Housekeeping "seal of approval." They give added assurance that a website is abiding by its posted privacy statement.

Privacy Seal Programs

Privacy seal programs offer third-party verification and monitoring of the information practices of websites. These programs have also established complaint and resolution procedures for users who believe that their privacy has been violated by a program participant.

The TRUSTe Privacy Seal Program

TRUSTe is an independent, non-profit initiative working to build consumer trust and confidence on the Internet. TRUSTe is responsible for developing the first online privacy seal program. The TRUSTe privacy seal program assures consumers that the websites they visit are compliant with fair information practices approved by the U.S. Department of Commerce, the Federal Trade Commission and prominent industry-represented organizations and associations.

A copy of the Code of Information Practices is set forth at Appendix 18 of this almanac.

A website that is a member of the TRUSTe seal program will display a TRUSTe privacy seal on the website's privacy statement. As further discussed in Chapter 7 of this almanac, TRUSTe also sponsors The TRUSTe Children's Privacy Seal for websites that are directed at children under 13.

When the user clicks on the privacy seal, they will be directed to a validation page on the TRUSTe website. If the user is not directed to the validation page, the user should be aware that the website may be displaying a fraudulent TRUSTe seal. To verify that the website is a member of the TRUSTe seal program, they can view a list of participants on the TRUSTe website at:

http://www.truste.com/users/users_lookup.html.

If a user believes that a TRUSTe participant has committed a privacy violation, an online complaint—referred to as a "watchdog"—should be filed with TRUSTe at:

http://www.truste.com/users/users_watchdog_intro.html.

TRUSTe will review the complaint and confirm that the website is a TRUSTe participant. TRUSTe can only act on privacy violation complaints, and can only accept complaints about a company that is a participant in the program. TRUSTe will then contact the website and make inquiries about the complaint. TRUSTe may also contact the user to get more information about their complaint. TRUSTe will contact the participating company and respond to the user within 10 business days. The participating company has 5 days after that to respond to TRUSTe and the user.

Depending on the nature of the complaint, TRUSTe may require the participating company to change its stated privacy policy or privacy practices. TRUSTe will also have the user's information corrected, modified, or deleted, as appropriate. A company that refuses to comply with a TRUSTe decision may be referred to the appropriate government agency, removed from the TRUSTe program, and be subject to legal action with TRUSTe. Either party to the complaint may file an appeal of a TRUSTe decision within 10 days of receipt of the decision.

BBBOnline Privacy Seal Program

BBBOnline is a wholly owned subsidiary of the Council of Better Business Bureaus. BBBOnline also operates a privacy seal program which requires its website participants to exercise responsible privacy practices.

A website that is a BBBOnline participant will display a privacy seal on the website's homepage or on its privacy statement. The seal provides a link to the validation page of the BBBOnline website. To verify that the website is a member of the BBBOnline seal program, the user can view a list of participants on the BBBOnline website at:

http://www.bbbonline.org/search/Pribrowse.asp.

Before filing a complaint with BBBOnline, users are asked to review the eligibility criteria posted on their website at:

http://www.bbbonline.com/consumer/criteria.asp.

Users are also advised to make a good faith effort to contact the website operator before filing the complaint. If the user cannot reach a satisfactory resolution with the website, they can file the complaint online at:

http://www.bbbonline.org/consumer/complaint.asp.

BBBOnline will review the complaint. Users are asked to include the following items with their complaint:

1. A copy of all correspondence between the user and the organization or company that operates the website.

2. Information for identification purposes.

3. Information about which included materials are confidential and which are not.

BBBOnline will determine the eligibility of the complaint, and evaluate, investigate, analyze, and make a decision about how to resolve the complaint. The complaint will be forwarded to the website for its comments, and will also contact both parties if it needs additional information.

The website has 15 business days to respond to the complaint. Once the answer is received, it is forwarded to the user, who has 10 days to submit any additional information. The reply is then forwarded to the website, which has an additional 10 days to reply. After all information is submitted, a decision will be rendered.

Depending on the nature of the complaint, BBBOnline may require the participating company to change its stated privacy policy or privacy practices. BBBOnline will also have the user's information corrected, modified, or deleted, as appropriate. A company that refuses to comply with a BBBOnline decision may be referred to the appropriate government agency, removed from the BBBOnline program, and be subject to legal action with BBBOnline.

BBBOnLine also provides an appeals process for matters involving substantial questions or interpretations of BBBOnLine privacy standards, or in situations where there is a significant possibility that the matter might be decided differently.

The WebTrust Privacy Program

The WebTrust Privacy Program was developed by the public accounting profession. The WebTrust On-line Privacy seal displayed on a website indicates that an accountant has independently verified that the business abides by its privacy commitments.

Personally identifiable information such as the user's name, address, e-mail address, and credit card information are covered by the WebTrust program. WebTrust requires that the business advise the consumer what information is being gathered, how it will be used, how the consumer can correct inaccurate information, and how they can "opt out."

WebTrust standards demand that the website discloses and complies with its on-line privacy practices. However, WebTrust does not provide a dispute resolution process for consumers.

THE PRIVACY PARTNERSHIP

The Privacy Partnership is an ongoing education effort designed to raise business and consumer awareness to the privacy issue. The Privacy partnership was initiated in 1998 by TRUSTe, together with a coalition of businesses seeking to implement an industry-wide approach to privacy education. Each of the participating websites donates banner ad space designed to educate the public about privacy issues.

The initial goal of the Privacy Partnership was to raise awareness about privacy and to encourage websites to post privacy statements. The proliferation of online privacy statements and privacy seal program partici-pants indicates that these early goals have been successful. The Privacy Partnership has now focused its efforts on educating consumers on all of the resources available to ensure privacy protection. As the internet ex-pands and privacy concerns grow, the Privacy Partnership is dedicated to teaching consumers and businesses about online privacy.

CHAPTER 6:
ONLINE FINANCIAL SERVICES

INTERNET BANKING

Internet banking is a rapidly growing technology available through many banks. The service is generally offered to the customer for free or at a small monthly charge. Studies have indicated that there is substantial customer demand for these services and banks may have to offer this service in order to stay competitive. Over thirty-five million households are connected to the Internet and the traffic doubles every 100 days. According to the Gartner Group Inc., the number of U.S. households banking online will grow to 24.2 million by 2004.

Unfortunately, Internet banking customers must necessarily divulge a lot of their personal identifying and financial information in order to participate. In order to sign up for Internet banking, the customer accesses their bank's website and follows the procedure for setting up the online banking account. After providing the account number and other identifying information, the customer is generally asked to choose a username and a password which they will use to access their existing accounts electronically.

Once registered, the customer can generally view their bank statements online, including recent activity, download their statements to their computer, and view imaged copies of individual items, without having to wait for their statements in the mail. In addition, most banks also offer the customer the ability to view the long-term activity on their account. The customer may also be able to link all of their bank accounts, transfer funds between accounts, open new accounts, apply for loans, order checks, make investments, and pay bills online.

Unfortunately, identity thieves who are able to obtain the consumer's username and password are also able to access this wealth of information and services. Further, if the website is not secure, as set forth above, identity thieves who are knowledgeable computer hackers may be able to access information through the bank's website.

Consumers should safeguard their Internet banking password very carefully. It is just as valuable as the PIN number assigned to the consumer's ATM card. Don't use a password that can easily be guessed by an identity thief. It is also wise to change your password from time to time to minimize the risk that your account will be accessed. In addition, if you get an e-mail asking you to confirm your password, do not respond without calling the bank directly.

Given the extensive amount of personal identifying and financial information involved in Internet banking, there are serious concerns relating to security issues, thus banks are very careful in selecting and developing an appropriate software system with a secure online server to process their customer's banking transactions. Customers should inquire about the bank's online security procedures to make sure that their information is secure and the risk of interception by identity thieves is minimized.

THE GRAMM-LEACH-BLILEY ACT (GLBA)

The Gramm-Leach-Bliley Act (GLBA) requires financial institutions to ensure the security and confidentiality of the personal information financial institutions collect from their customers, such as their names, addresses and phone numbers; bank and credit card account numbers; income and credit histories; and social security numbers.

Safeguarding the personal identifying information of customers is particularly important insofar as so much banking and investment activity is now conducted over the Internet, which can present significant privacy and security challenges.

THE SAFEGUARDS RULE

As part of its implementation of the GLBA, the Federal Trade Commission (FTC) has issued the Safeguards Rule. The Safeguards Rule requires financial institutions under FTC jurisdiction to secure customer records and information.

The text of the Safeguards Rule is set forth at Appendix 19 of this almanac.

Covered Institutions

The Safeguards Rule applies to businesses, regardless of size, that are "significantly engaged" in providing financial products or services to consumers. This includes check-cashing businesses, data processors, mortgage brokers, nonbank lenders, personal property or real estate appraisers, professional tax prepares, courier services, and retailers that issue credit cards to consumers.

The Safeguards Rule also applies to financial companies, like credit reporting agencies and ATM operators, that receive information from other financial institutions about their customers. In addition to developing their own safeguards, financial institutions are responsible for taking steps to ensure that their affiliates and service providers safeguard customer information in their care. Poorly-managed customer data can lead to identity theft which occurs when someone steals a consumer's personal identifying information for illegal purposes, e.g., to fraudulently open new charge accounts, order merchandise or borrow money.

Requirements

The Safeguards Rule requires financial institutions to develop a written information security plan that describes their program to protect customer information. The plan must be appropriate to the financial institution's size and complexity, the nature and scope of its activities, and the sensitivity of the customer information it handles. As part of its plan, each financial institution must:

1. Designate one or more employees to coordinate the safeguards;

2. Identify and assess the risks to customer information in each relevant area of the company's operation, and evaluate the effectiveness of the current safeguards for controlling these risks;

3. Design and implement a safeguards program, and regularly monitor and test it;

4. Select appropriate service providers and contract with them to implement safeguards; and

5. Evaluate and adjust the program in light of relevant circumstances, including changes in the firm's business arrangements or operations, or the results of testing and monitoring of safeguards.

Each financial institution is advised to implement safeguards appropriate to its own circumstances. For example, some financial institutions may choose to describe their safeguards programs in a single document, while others may set forth their plans in several different documents, such as one to cover an information technology division and another to describe the training program for employees.

Similarly, a company may decide to designate a single employee to coordinate safeguards or may spread this responsibility among several employees who will work together. In addition, a firm with a small staff may design and implement a more limited employee training program than a firm with a large number of employees. A financial institution that doesn't receive or store any information online may take fewer steps to assess risks to its computers than a firm that routinely conducts its business online.

When a firm implements safeguards, the Safeguards Rule requires it to consider all areas of its operation. According to the FTC, the following three areas are particularly important to information security:

Employee Management and Training

The success or failure of a company's information security plan depends largely on the employees who implement it. Therefore, it is important to carefully check the references of all potential employees who will have access to customer information. In addition, new employees should be required to sign an agreement acknowledging their responsibility for following the company's confidentiality and security standards for handling customer information. Further, access to customer information should be limited to employees who have a business reason for having the information.

Employees should be properly trained in maintaining the security, confidentiality and integrity of customer information. The FTC advises businesses to take the following steps to ensure the security of customer information:

1. Locking rooms and file cabinets where paper records are kept;

2. Using password-activated screensavers;

3. Using strong passwords which are at least eight characters long;

4. Changing passwords periodically, and not posting passwords near employees' computers;

5. Encrypting sensitive customer information when it is transmitted electronically over networks or stored online;

6. Referring calls or other requests for customer information to designated individuals who have had safeguards training; and

7. Recognizing any fraudulent attempt to obtain customer information and reporting it to appropriate law enforcement agencies.

Information Systems

Information systems include network and software design, and information processing, storage, transmission, retrieval, and disposal. Security should be maintained throughout the life cycle of customer information—i.e., from data entry to data disposal. The FTC advises businesses to take steps to ensure that customer information remains secure, as set forth below.

Storage of Information

Customer information should be stored in a secure manner. For example:

1. Paper records should be stored in a secure area which can only be accessed by authorized employees;

2. Electronic customer information should be stored on a secure server that is accessible only with a password or other security protection;

3. Sensitive customer data should not be stored on a machine with an Internet connection; and

4. Backup files should be securely maintained, e.g., by storing off-line or in a physically secure area.

Retrieval and Transmission of Information

When collecting or transmitting customer information, data transmission should be secure. For example:

1. When collecting credit card information or other sensitive financial data, a Secure Sockets Layer (SSL) or other secure connection should be used so that the information is encrypted in transit.

2. When collecting information directly from consumers, secure transmission should be automatic and customers should be cautioned against transmitting sensitive data, such as their account numbers, by e-mail; and

3. When transmitting sensitive data by e-mail, messages should be password protected so that only authorized employees have access to the information.

Disposal of Information

Customer information should be disposed of in a secure manner. For example:

1. A records retention manager should be designated to supervise the disposal of records containing nonpublic personal information.

2. Customer information recorded on paper should be shredded or recycled and stored in a secure area until picked up by a recycling service.

3. When disposing of computers, diskettes, magnetic tapes, hard drives or any other electronic media, all data that contains customer information should be erased.

4. Hardware should be effectively destroyed.

5. Outdated customer information should be disposed of promptly.

Managing System Failures

Effective security management includes the prevention, detection and response to attacks, intrusions or other system failures. The FTC advises businesses to take the following steps to effectively manage their information systems:

1. Maintain and follow a written contingency plan to address any breaches of physical, administrative or technical safeguards.

2. Check with software vendors regularly to obtain and install patches that resolve software vulnerabilities.

3. Use anti-virus software that updates automatically.

4. Maintain up-to-date firewalls, particularly if the business uses broadband Internet access or allows employees to connect to the computer network from home or at other off-site locations.

5. Provide central management of security tools for employees and pass along updates about any security risks or breaches.

6. Take steps to preserve the security, confidentiality and integrity of customer information in the event of a computer or other technological failure, e.g., back up all customer data regularly.

7. Maintain systems and procedures to ensure that access to nonpublic consumer information is granted only to legitimate and valid users, e.g. by using passwords combined with personal identifiers to authenticate the identity of customers.

8. Notify customers promptly if their nonpublic personal information is subject to loss, damage or unauthorized access.

THE FINANCIAL SERVICES MODERNIZATION ACT

A new federal law, the Financial Services Modernization Act, gives consumers some rights to protect their personal financial information. It outlines the circumstances when financial service companies must allow the consumer to limit the sharing of their information, and outlines the steps consumers must take to do so. As a result of this new law, consumers will periodically receive notices from the financial institutions with which they do business, notifying them of the company's privacy policy.

CHAPTER 7:
PROTECTING CHILDREN'S PRIVACY ONLINE

IN GENERAL

Children encompass one of the largest groups of Internet users. Approximately 30 million American children under 18 currently use the Internet, and more than 40 million are expected to be online by 2005. Children use the Internet to access a wealth of information to help them with their schoolwork, as well as for entertainment and communication purposes.

The Internet provides many educational advantages for children that earlier generations could not have imagined. However, along with these benefits, there are serious concerns about online privacy and safety for children. Although children learn how to use computers at a very early age, they still lack maturity and judgment, which may lead them to reveal personal information that should not be revealed.

WEBSITES

When a child registers on a website, that site often requests the child to provide personal information, such as their name, address, e-mail address, preferences about products, favorite activities, etc. The information collected may be used in other areas of the website, such as member profiles and chat rooms. The information may also be used to create a customer list. Customer lists are often sold to brokers, who may then sell the list to an advertiser.

When a child's personal information is disseminated, it may enable others to contact the child. There have been a number of cases where children have been contacted online by potential child molesters who try and gain the child's confidence with bad intentions. Some of these online conversations have led to personal contact, sexual molestation, and murder.

Therefore, parents are advised to oversee their children's online activities, including the websites they visit and the individuals with whom they communicate. The importance of privacy online should be emphasized and they should be advised not to give out their name and address when communicating in chat rooms or on message boards.

Since it is impossible to constantly monitor a child's online activity, it is important to make sure the child cannot visit sites that are unsuitable for children. Parental controls are available through the internet service provider. These controls allow the parent to place restrictions on the websites a child is allowed to access and the amount of unsolicited e-mail a child may receive. It is also important to review any links on the website that might forward the child to another website that you may not want your child to visit.

In addition, it is crucial for parents to require their children to obtain permission before giving out personal information online, including their name, address or any other information about them or their family. If you become aware of a website that is collecting information from children without requiring parental consent, an online complaint may be made to the Federal Trade Commission (FTC) at kidsprivacy@ftc.gov.

PRIVACY STATEMENTS

It is important to read the privacy statement of any website your child may visit in order to determine exactly how the child's personal information may be used. The privacy statement explains how the website users the information collected from its visitors. If a website does not have a privacy policy, it is best not to patronize that website. As further explained in Chapter 5 of this almanac, the privacy statement is a legally binding document.

Parents and children should read the privacy statement together and the child should be taught the meaning of its content. The privacy statement of any website that is linked should also be reviewed. The privacy statement should explain how a parent can review, change or delete any information that the website has collected from their child.

THE TRUSTE CHILDREN'S PRIVACY SEAL

As set forth in Chapter 5, TRUSTe is a nonprofit third-party oversight program that regularly monitors the adherence of websites to their privacy statements. TRUSTe has the power to enforce compliance with its program.

The TRUSTEe Children's Privacy Seal is a trustmark awarded only to websites that adhere to established privacy principles of disclosure, choice, access and security. The TRUSTEe seal means that the particular website is dedicated to protecting the child's online privacy, and that the user has the ability to control how their personal information is used by that website.

The TRUSTe Children's Privacy Seal is a seal for webites that are directed at children under 13. Every website displaying the TRUSTe Children's Seal must:

1. Adhere to the privacy principles of notice, choice, access and security.

2. Obtain verifiable parental consent before collecting personally identifiable information from a child.

3. Allow a parent to access and delete a child's personal information at any time.

The TRUSTe Children's Seal on a website also means that the site can be trusted to abide by the guarantees it gives in its privacy statement. Generally, the privacy statement can be accessed by clicking on the privacy seal.

If a parent believes their child's privacy has been violated on a website displaying the TRUSTe Children's Seal, they are advised to contact TRUSTe directly by registering a complaint on their website at: www.truste.org/users/users_watchdog.html.

THE CHILDREN'S ONLINE PRIVACY PROTECTION ACT (COPPA)

In the past, a number of websites were encouraging children to provide personal information about themselves or their family for their own marketing purposes without obtaining parental consent. Some of these websites enticed children with games and free gifts. In response to this kind of activity, Congress passed the Children's Online Privacy Protection Act in October 1998.

The implementing rules for the Act set forth by the Federal Trade Commission (FTC) took effect April 21, 2000. The primary goal of the Act is to place parents in control over what information is collected from their children online. Websites directed at children under 13 are legally required to protect the privacy of children under the rules of COPPA. The COPPA requires companies to gain parental consent before collecting personal information from children under 13 years old.

The COPPA applies to individually identifiable information about a child such as name, home address, e-mail address, telephone number or any other information that would allow someone to identify or contact the child. The Act also covers other types of information, such as hobbies, interests and information collected through cookies or other types of tracking mechanisms when they are tied to individually identifiable information.

The COPPA applies to operators of commercial websites and online services directed to children under 13 that collect personal information from children, and operators of general audience sites with actual knowledge that they are collecting information from children under 13.

The COPPA sets out a number of factors in determining whether a website is targeted to children, such as the website's (i) subject matter; (ii) language; (iii) whether it uses animated characters; and (iv) whether advertising appearing on the site is directed to children. The FTC will also consider empirical evidence regarding the ages of the site's visitors. These standards are very similar to those previously established for TV, radio, and print advertising.

The COPPA requires the website operator to post a link to a notice of its information practices on the home page of its website or online service and at each area where it collects personal information from children. An operator of a general audience site with a separate children's area must post a link to its notice on the home page of the children's area.

The link to the privacy notice must be clear and prominent. The notice must be clearly written and understandable. It should not include any unrelated or confusing materials. It must state the following information:

1. The name and contact information, including address, telephone number and e-mail address, of all operators collecting or maintaining children's personal information through the Web site or online service. If more than one operator is collecting information at the site, the site may select and provide contact information for only one operator who will respond to all inquiries from parents about the site's privacy policies. However, the names of all operators must be listed in the notice.

2. The kinds of personal information collected from children and how the information is collected—directly from the child or passively, e.g., through cookies.

3. How the operator uses the personal information.

4. Whether the operator discloses information collected from children to third parties. If so, the operator also must disclose the kinds of businesses in which the third parties are engaged; the general purposes for which the information is used; and whether the third parties have agreed to maintain the confidentiality and security of the information.

5. That the parent has the option to agree to the collection and use of the child's information without consenting to the disclosure of the information to third parties.

6. That the operator may not require a child to disclose more information than is reasonably necessary to participate in an activity as a condition of participation.

7. That the parent can review the child's personal information, ask to have it deleted and refuse to allow any further collection or use of the child's information. The notice also must state the procedures for the parent to follow.

The notice to parents must contain the same information included on the notice on the website. In addition, an operator must notify a parent that it wishes to collect personal information from the child, that the parent's consent is required for the collection, use and disclosure of the information, and how the parent can provide consent. The notice to parents must be written clearly and understandably, and must not contain any unrelated or confusing information. An operator may use any one of a number of methods to notify a parent, including sending an e-mail message to the parent or a notice by postal mail.

Before collecting, using or disclosing personal information from a child, an operator must obtain verifiable parental consent from the child's parent. This means an operator must make reasonable efforts to ensure that before personal information is collected from a child, a parent of the child receives notice of the operator's information practices and consents to those practices.

Operators may use e-mail to get parental consent for all internal uses of personal information, such as marketing back to a child based on his or her preferences or communicating promotional updates about site content, as long as they take additional steps to increase the likelihood that the parent has, in fact, provided the consent.

An operator must give a parent the option to agree to the collection and use of the child's personal information without agreeing to the disclosure of the information to third parties. However, when a parent agrees to the collection and use of their child's personal information, the operator may release that information to others who use it solely to provide support for the internal operations of the website or service, including technical support and order fulfillment.

The regulations include several exceptions that allow operators to collect a child's e-mail address without getting the parent's consent in advance. These exceptions cover many popular online activities for kids, including contests, online newsletters, homework help and electronic postcards. Prior parental consent is not required when:

1. An operator collects a child's or parent's e-mail address to provide notice and seek consent;

2. An operator collects an e-mail address to respond to a one-time request from a child and then deletes it;

3. An operator collects an e-mail address to respond more than once to a specific request in which case the operator must notify the parent that it is communicating regularly with the child and give the parent the opportunity to stop the communication before sending or delivering a second communication to a child;

4. An operator collects a child's name or online contact information to protect the safety of a child who is participating on the site in which case the operator must notify the parent and give him or her the opportunity to prevent further use of the information;

5. An operator collects a child's name or online contact information to protect the security or liability of the site or to respond to law enforcement, if necessary, and does not use it for any other purpose.

An operator is required to send a new notice and request for consent to parents if there are material changes in the collection, use or disclosure practices to which the parent had previously agreed.

At a parent's request, operators must disclose the general kinds of personal information they collect online from children as well as the specific information collected from children who visit their sites. Operators must use reasonable procedures to ensure they are dealing with the child's parent before they provide access to the child's specific information. They can use a variety of methods to verify the parent's identity, including:

1. Obtaining a signed form from the parent via postal mail or facsimile;

2. Accepting and verifying a credit card number;

3. Taking calls from parents on a toll-free telephone number staffed by trained personnel;

4. E-mail accompanied by a digital signature;

5. E-mail accompanied by a PIN or password obtained through one of the verification methods above.

Operators who follow one of these procedures acting in good faith to a request for parental access are protected from liability under federal and state law for inadvertent disclosures of a child's information to someone who purports to be a parent.

At any time, a parent may revoke his/her consent, refuse to allow an operator to further use or collect their child's personal information, and direct the operator to delete the information. In turn, the operator may terminate any service provided to the child, but only if the information at issue is reasonably necessary for the child's participation in that activity. If other activities on the Web site do not require the child's e-mail address, the operator must allow the child access to those activities.

The FTC monitors the Internet for compliance with the Rule and brings law enforcement actions where appropriate to deter violations. Parents and others can submit complaints to the FTC for violations of COPPA, as set forth in Chapter 2 of this almanac.

The FTC may impose civil penalties for violations of the Rule in the same manner as for other Rules under the FTC Act. The level of penalties assessed may turn on a number of factors including egregiousness of the violation, e.g., the number of children involved, the amount and type of personal information collected, how the information was used, whether it was shared with third parties and the size of the company.

The FTC has set up a special Web page designed for children, parents, businesses, and educators at http://www.ftc.gov/kidzprivacy. In addition to providing compliance materials for businesses and parents, this Web page features online safety tips for children and other useful educational resources about the Children's Online Privacy Protection Act and related rules and online privacy in general.

The text of the Children's Online Privacy Protection Act (COPPA) is set forth at Appendix 20 of this almanac.

APPENDIX 1:
THE ELECTRONIC COMMUNICATIONS PRIVACY ACT

TITLE 18. CRIMES AND CRIMINAL PROCEDURE

PART I—CRIMES

CHAPTER 119—WIRE AND ELECTRONIC COMMUNICATIONS INTERCEPTION AND INTERCEPTION OF ORAL COMMUNICATIONS

Sec. 2510. Definitions.

As used in this chapter—

(1) "wire communication" means any aural transfer made in whole or in part through the use of facilities for the transmission of communications by the aid of wire, cable, or other like connection between the point of origin and the point of reception (including the use of such connection in a switching station) furnished or operated by any person engaged in providing or operating such facilities for the transmission of interstate or foreign communications for communications affecting interstate or foreign commerce and such term includes any electronic storage of such communication;

(2) "oral communication" means any oral communication uttered by a person exhibiting an expectation that such communication is not subject to interception under circumstances justifying such expectation, but such term does not include any electronic communication;

(3) "State" means any State of the United States, the District of Columbia, the Commonwealth of Puerto Rico, and any territory or possession of the United States;

(4) "intercept" means the aural or other acquisition of the contents of any wire, electronic, or oral communication through the use of any electronic, mechanical, or other device;

(5) "electronic, mechanical, or other device" means any device or apparatus which can be used to intercept a wire, oral, or electronic communication other than—

(a) any telephone or telegraph instrument, equipment or facility, or any component thereof, (i) furnished to the subscriber or user by a provider of wire or electronic communication service in the ordinary course of its business and being used by the subscriber or user in the ordinary course of its business or furnished by such subscriber or user for connection to the facilities of such service and used in the ordinary course of its business; or (ii) being used by a provider of wire or electronic communication service in the ordinary course of its business, or by an investigative or law enforcement officer in the ordinary course of his duties;

(b) a hearing aid or similar device being used to correct subnormal hearing to not better than normal;

(6) "person" means any employee, or agent of the United States or any State or political subdivision thereof, and any individual, partnership, association, joint stock company, trust, or corporation;

(7) "Investigative or law enforcement officer" means any officer of the United States or of a State or political subdivision thereof, who is empowered by law to conduct investigations of or to make arrests for offenses enumerated in this chapter, and any attorney authorized by law to prosecute or participate in the prosecution of such offenses;

(8) "contents", when used with respect to any wire, oral, or electronic communication, includes any information concerning the substance, purport, or meaning of that communication;

(9) "Judge of competent jurisdiction" means—

(a) a judge of a United States district court or a United States court of appeals; and

(b) a judge of any court of general criminal jurisdiction of a State who is authorized by a statute of that State to enter orders authorizing interceptions of wire, oral, or electronic communications;

(10) "communication common carrier" shall have the same meaning which is given the term "common carrier" by section 153(h) of title 47 of the United States Code;

(11) "aggrieved person" means a person who was a party to any intercepted wire, oral, or electronic communication or a person against whom the interception was directed;

(12) "electronic communication" means any transfer of signs, signals, writing, images, sounds, data, or intelligence of any nature transmitted in whole or in part by a wire, radio, electromagnetic, photoelectronic or photooptical system that affects interstate or foreign commerce, but does not include—

(A) any wire or oral communication;

(B) any communication made through a tone-only paging device; or

(C) any communication from a tracking device (as defined in section 3117 of this title);

(13) "user" means any person or entity who—

(A) uses an electronic communication service; and

(B) is duly authorized by the provider of such service;

(14) "electronic communications system" means any wire, radio, electromagnetic, photooptical or photoelectronic facilities for the transmission of electronic communications, and any computer facilities or related electronic equipment for the electronic storage of such communications;

(15) "electronic communication service" means any service which provides to users thereof the ability to send or receive wire or electronic communications;

(16) "readily accessible to the general public" means, with respect to a radio communication, that such communication is not—

(A) scrambled or encrypted;

(B) transmitted using modulation techniques whose essential parameters have been withheld from the public with the intention of preserving the privacy of such communication;

(C) carried on a subcarrier or other signal subsidiary to a radio transmission;

(D) transmitted over a communication system provided by a common carrier, unless the communication is a tone only paging system communication;

(E) transmitted on frequencies allocated under part 25, subpart D, E, or F of part 74, or part 94 of the Rules of the Federal Communications Commission, unless, in the case of a communication transmitted on a frequency allocated under part 74 that is not exclusively allocated to broadcast auxiliary services, the communication is a two-way voice communication by radio; or

(F) an electronic communication;

(17) "electronic storage" means—

(A) any temporary, intermediate storage of a wire or electronic communication incidental to the electronic transmission thereof; and

(B) any storage of such communication by an electronic communication service for purposes of backup protection of such communication; and

(18) "aural transfer" means a transfer containing the human voice at any point between and including the point of origin and the point of reception.

Sec. 2511. Interception and disclosure of wire, oral, or electronic communications prohibited.

(1) Except as otherwise specifically provided in this chapter any person who—

(a) intentionally intercepts, endeavors to intercept, or procures any other person to intercept or endeavor to intercept, any wire, oral, or electronic communication;

(b) intentionally uses, endeavors to use, or procures any other person to use or endeavor to use any electronic, mechanical, or other device to intercept any oral communication when—

(i) such device is affixed to, or otherwise transmits a signal through, a wire, cable, or other like connection used in wire communication; or

(ii) such device transmits communications by radio, or interferes with the transmission of such communication; or

(iii) such person knows, or has reason to know, that such device or any component thereof has been sent through the mail or transported in interstate or foreign commerce; or

(iv) such use or endeavor to use (A) takes place on the premises of any business or other commercial establishment the operations of which affect interstate or foreign commerce; or (B) obtains or is for the purpose of obtaining information relating to the operations of any business or other commercial establishment the operations of which affect interstate or foreign commerce; or

(v) such person acts in the District of Columbia, the Commonwealth of Puerto Rico, or any territory or possession of the United States;

(c) intentionally discloses, or endeavors to disclose, to any other person the contents of any wire, oral, or electronic communication, knowing or having reason to know that the information was obtained through the interception of a wire, oral, or electronic communication in violation of this subsection; or

(d) intentionally uses, or endeavors to use, the contents of any wire, oral, or electronic communication, knowing or having reason to know that the information was obtained through the interception of a wire, oral, or electronic communication in violation of this subsection; shall be punished as provided in subsection (4) or shall be subject to suit as provided in subsection (5).

(2)(a)(i) It shall not be unlawful under this chapter for an operator of a switchboard, or on officer, employee, or agent of a provider of wire or electronic communication service, whose facilities are used in the transmission of a wire communication, to intercept, disclose, or use that communication in the normal course of his employment while engaged in any activity which is a necessary incident to the rendition of his service or to the protection of the rights or property of the provider of that service, except that a provider of wire communication service to the public shall not utilize service observing or random monitoring except for mechanical or service quality control checks.

(ii) Notwithstanding any other law, providers of wire or electronic communication service, their officers, employees, and agents, landlords, custodians, or other persons, are authorized to provide information, facilities, or technical assistance to persons authorized by law to intercept wire, oral, or electronic communications or to conduct electronic surveillance, as defined in section 101 of the Foreign Intelligence Surveillance Act of 1978, if such provider, its officers, employees, or agents, landlord, custodian, or other specified person, has been provided with—

(A) a court order directing such assistance signed by the authorizing judge, or

(B) a certification in writing by a person specified in section 2518(7) of this title or the Attorney General of the United States that no warrant or court order is required by law, that all statutory requirements have been met, and that the specified assistance is required, setting forth the period of time during which the provision of the information, facilities, or technical assistance is authorized and specifying the information, facilities, or technical assistance required. No provider of wire or electronic communication service, officer, employee, or agent thereof, or landlord, custodian, or other specified person shall disclose the existence of any interception or surveillance or the device used to accomplish the interception or surveillance with respect to which the person has been furnished a court order or certification under this chapter, except as may otherwise be required by legal process and then only after prior notification to the Attorney General or to the principal prosecuting attorney of a State or any political subdivision of a State, as may be appropriate. Any such disclosure, shall render such person liable for the civil damages provided for in section 2520. No cause of action shall lie in any court against any provider of wire or electronic communication service, its officers, employees, or agents, landlord, custodian, or other specified person for providing information, facilities, or assistance in accordance with the terms of a court order or certification under this chapter.

(b) It shall not be unlawful under this chapter for an officer, employee, or agent of the Federal Communications Commission, in the normal course of his employment and in discharge of the monitoring responsibilities exercised by the Commission in the enforcement of chapter 5 of title 47 of the United States Code, to intercept a wire or electronic communication, or oral communication transmitted by radio, or to disclose or use the information thereby obtained.

(c) It shall not be unlawful under this chapter for a person acting under color of law to intercept a wire, oral, or electronic communication, where such person is a party to the communication or one of the parties to the communication has given prior consent to such interception.

(d) It shall not be unlawful under this chapter for a person not acting under color of law to intercept a wire, oral, or electronic communication where such person is a party to the communication or where one of the parties to the communication has given prior consent to such interception unless such communication is intercepted for the purpose of committing any criminal or tortious act in violation of the Constitution or laws of the United States or of any State.

(e) Notwithstanding any other provision of this title or section 705 or 706 of the Communications Act of 1934, it shall not be unlawful for an officer, employee, or agent of the United States in the normal course of his official duty to conduct electronic surveillance, as defined in section 101 of the Foreign Intelligence Surveillance Act of 1978, as authorized by that Act.

(f) Nothing contained in this chapter or chapter 121, or section 705 of the Communications Act of 1934, shall be deemed to affect the acquisition by the United States Government of foreign intelligence information from international or foreign communications, or foreign intelligence activities conducted in accordance with otherwise applicable Federal law involving a foreign electronic communications system, utilizing a means other than electronic surveillance as defined in section 101 of the Foreign Intelligence Surveillance Act of 1978, and procedures in this chapter and the Foreign

Intelligence Surveillance Act of 1978 shall be the exclusive means by which electronic surveillance, as defined in section 101 of such Act, and the interception of domestic wire and oral communications may be conducted.

(g) It shall not be unlawful under this chapter or chapter 121 of this title for any person—

(i) to intercept or access an electronic communication made through an electronic communication system that is configured so that such electronic communication is readily accessible to the general public;

(ii) to intercept any radio communication which is transmitted—

(I) by any station for the use of the general public, or that relates to ships, aircraft, vehicles, or persons in distress;

(II) by any governmental, law enforcement, civil defense, private land mobile, or public safety communications system, including police and fire, readily accessible to the general public;

(III) by a station operating on an authorized frequency within the bands allocated to the amateur, citizens band, or general mobile radio services; or

(IV) by any marine or aeronautical communications system;

(iii) to engage in any conduct which—

(I) is prohibited by section 633 of the Communications Act of 1934; or

(II) is excepted from the application of section 705(a) of the Communications Act of 1934 by section 705(b) of that Act;

(iv) to intercept any wire or electronic communication the transmission of which is causing harmful interference to any lawfully operating station or consumer electronic equipment, to the extent necessary to identify the source of such interference; or

(v) for other users of the same frequency to intercept any radio communication made through a system that utilizes frequencies monitored by individuals engaged in the provision or the use of such system, if such communication is not scrambled or encrypted.

(h) It shall not be unlawful under this chapter—

(i) to use a pen register or a trap and trace device (as those terms are defined for the purposes of chapter 206 (relating to pen registers and trap and trace devices) of this title); or

(ii) for a provider of electronic communication service to record the fact that a wire or electronic communication was initiated or completed in order to protect such provider, another provider furnishing service toward the completion of the wire or electronic communication, or a user of that service, from fraudulent, unlawful or abusive use of such service.

(3)(a) Except as provided in paragraph (b) of this subsection, a person or entity providing an electronic communication service to the public shall not intentionally divulge the contents of any communication (other than one to such person or entity, or an agent thereof) while in transmission on that service to any person or entity other than an addressee or intended recipient of such communication or an agent of such addressee or intended recipient.

(b) A person or entity providing electronic communication service to the public may divulge the contents of any such communication—

(i) as otherwise authorized in section 2511(2)(a) or 2517 of this title;

(ii) with the lawful consent of the originator or any addressee or intended recipient of such communication;

(iii) to a person employed or authorized, or whose facilities are used, to forward such communication to its destination; or

(iv) which were inadvertently obtained by the service provider and which appear to pertain to the commission of a crime, if such divulgence is made to a law enforcement agency.

(4)(a) Except as provided in paragraph (b) of this subsection or in subsection (5), whoever violates subsection (1) of this section shall be fined under this title or imprisoned not more than five years, or both.

(b) If the offense is a first offense under paragraph (a) of this subsection and is not for a tortious or illegal purpose or for purposes of direct or indirect commercial advantage or private commercial gain, and the wire or electronic communication with respect to which the offense under paragraph (a) is a radio communication that is not scrambled or encrypted, then—

(i) if the communication is not the radio portion of a cellular telephone communication, a public land mobile radio service communication or a paging service communication, and the conduct is not that described in subsection (5), the offender shall be fined under this title or imprisoned not more than one year, or both; and

(ii) if the communication is the radio portion of a cellular telephone communication, a public land mobile radio service communication or a paging service communication, the offender shall be fined not more than $500.

(c) Conduct otherwise an offense under this subsection that consists of or relates to the interception of a satellite transmission that is not encrypted or scrambled and that is transmitted—

(i) to a broadcasting station for purposes of retransmission to the general public; or

(ii) as an audio subcarrier intended for redistribution to facilities open to the public, but not including data transmissions or telephone calls, is not an offense under this subsection unless the conduct is for the purposes of direct or indirect commercial advantage or private financial gain.

(5)(a)(i) If the communication is—

(A) a private satellite video communication that is not scrambled or encrypted and the conduct in violation of this chapter is the private viewing of that communication and is not for a tortious or illegal purpose or for purposes of direct or indirect commercial advantage or private commercial gain; or

(B) a radio communication that is transmitted on frequencies allocated under subpart D of part 74 of the rules of the Federal Communications Commission that is not scrambled or encrypted and the conduct in violation of this chapter is not for a tortious or illegal purpose or for purposes of direct or indirect commercial advantage or private commercial gain, then the person who engages in such conduct shall be subject to suit by the Federal Government in a court of competent jurisdiction.

(ii) In an action under this subsection—

(A) if the violation of this chapter is a first offense for the person under paragraph (a) of subsection (4) and such person has not been found liable in a civil action under section 2520 of this title, the Federal Government shall be entitled to appropriate injunctive relief; and

(B) if the violation of this chapter is a second or subsequent offense under paragraph (a) of subsection (4) or such person has been found liable in any prior civil action under section 2520, the person shall be subject to a mandatory $500 civil fine.

(b) The court may use any means within its authority to enforce an injunction issued under paragraph (ii)(A), and shall impose a civil fine of not less than $500 for each violation of such an injunction.

Sec. 2520. Recovery of civil damages authorized.

(a) In general. Except as provided in section 2511(2)(a)(ii), any person whose wire, oral, or electronic communication is intercepted, disclosed, or intentionally used in violation of this chapter may in a civil action recover from the person or entity which engaged in that violation such relief as may be appropriate.

(b) Relief. In an action under this section, appropriate relief includes—

(1) such preliminary and other equitable or declaratory relief as may be appropriate;

(2) damages under subsection (c) and punitive damages in appropriate cases; and

(3) a reasonable attorney's fee and other litigation costs reasonably incurred.

(c) Computation of damages.

(1) In an action under this section, if the conduct in violation of this chapter is the private viewing of a private satellite video communication that is not scrambled or encrypted or if the communication is a radio communication that is transmitted on frequencies allocated under subpart D of part 74 of the rules of the Federal Communications Commission that is not scrambled or encrypted and the conduct is not for a tortious or illegal purpose or for purposes of direct or indirect commercial advantage or private commercial gain, then the court shall assess damages as follows:

(A) If the person who engaged in that conduct has not previously been enjoined under section 2511(5) and has not been found liable in a prior civil action under this section, the court shall assess the greater of the sum of actual damages suffered by the plaintiff, or statutory damages of not less than $50 and not more than $500.

(B) If, on one prior occasion, the person who engaged in that conduct has been enjoined under section 2511(5) or has been found liable in a civil action under this section, the court shall assess the greater of the sum of actual damages suffered by the plaintiff, or statutory damages of not less than $100 and not more than $1000.

(2) In any other action under this section, the court may assess as damages whichever is the greater of

(A) the sum of the actual damages suffered by the plaintiff and any profits made by the violator as a result of the violation; or

(B) statutory damages of whichever is the greater of $100 a day for each day of violation or $10,000.

(d) Defense. A good faith reliance on—

(1) a court warrant or order, a grand jury subpoena, a legislative authorization, or a statutory authorization;

(2) a request of an investigative or law enforcement officer under section 2518(7) of this title; or

(3) a good faith determination that section 2511(3) of this title permitted the conduct complained of; is a complete defense against any civil or criminal action brought under this chapter or any other law.

(e) Limitation. A civil action under this section may not be commenced later than two years after the date upon which the claimant first has a reasonable opportunity to discover the violation.

APPENDIX 2:
THE PRIVACY PROTECTION ACT OF 1980

[42 U.S.C. 2000AA]

SEC. 2000AA.—SEARCHES AND SEIZURES BY GOVERNMENT OFFICERS AND EMPLOYEES IN CONNECTION WITH INVESTIGATION OR PROSECUTION OF CRIMINAL OFFENSES

(a) Work product materials

Notwithstanding any other law, it shall be unlawful for a government officer or employee, in connection with the investigation or prosecution of a criminal offense, to search for or seize any work product materials possessed by a person reasonably believed to have a purpose to disseminate to the public a newspaper, book, broadcast, or other similar form of public communication, in or affecting interstate or foreign commerce; but this provision shall not impair or affect the ability of any government officer or employee, pursuant to otherwise applicable law, to search for or seize such materials, if—

> (1) there is probable cause to believe that the person possessing such materials has committed or is committing the criminal offense to which the materials relate: Provided, however, That a government officer or employee may not search for or seize such materials under the provisions of this paragraph if the offense to which the materials relate consists of the receipt, possession, communication, or withholding of such materials or the information contained therein (but such a search or seizure may be conducted under the provisions of this paragraph if the offense consists of the receipt, possession, or communication of information relating to the national defense, classified information, or restricted data under the provisions of section 793, 794, 797, or 798 of title 18, or section 2274, 2275, or 2277 of this title, or section 783 of title 50, or if the offense involves the production, possession, receipt, mailing, sale, distribution, shipment, or transportation of child pornography, the sexual exploitation of children, or the sale or purchase of children under section 2251, 2251A, 2252, or 2252A of title 18); or

(2) there is reason to believe that the immediate seizure of such materials is necessary to prevent the death of, or serious bodily injury to, a human being.

Notwithstanding any other law, it shall be unlawful for a government officer or employee, in connection with the investigation or prosecution of a criminal offense, to search for or seize documentary materials, other than work product materials, possessed by a person in connection with a purpose to disseminate to the public a newspaper, book, broadcast, or other similar form of public communication, in or affecting interstate or foreign commerce; but this provision shall not impair or affect the ability of any government officer or employee, pursuant to otherwise applicable law, to search for or seize such materials, if—

(1) there is probable cause to believe that the person possessing such materials has committed or is committing the criminal offense to which the materials relate: Provided, however, That a government officer or employee may not search for or seize such materials under the provisions of this paragraph if the offense to which the materials relate consists of the receipt, possession, communication, or withholding of such materials or the information contained therein (but such a search or seizure may be conducted under the provisions of this paragraph if the offense consists of the receipt, possession, or communication of information relating to the national defense, classified information, or restricted data under the provisions of section 793, 794, 797, or 798 of title 18, or section 2274, 2275, or 2277 of this title, or section 783 of title 50, or if the offense involves the production, possession, receipt, mailing, sale, distribution, shipment, or transportation of child pornography, the sexual exploitation of children, or the sale or purchase of children under section 2251, 2251A, 2252, or 2252A of title 18);

(2) there is reason to believe that the immediate seizure of such materials is necessary to prevent the death of, or serious bodily injury to, a human being;

(3) there is reason to believe that the giving of notice pursuant to a subpena duces tecum would result in the destruction, alteration, or concealment of such materials; or

(4) such materials have not been produced in response to a court order directing compliance with a subpena duces tecum, and—

(A) all appellate remedies have been exhausted; or

(B) there is reason to believe that the delay in an investigation or trial occasioned by further proceedings relating to the subpena would threaten the interests of justice.

(c) Objections to court ordered subpoenas; affidavits

In the event a search warrant is sought pursuant to paragraph (4)(B) of subsection (b) of this section, the person possessing the materials shall be afforded adequate opportunity to submit an affidavit setting forth the basis for any contention that the materials sought are not subject to seizure.

APPENDIX 3:
THE USA PATRIOT ACT
(H.R.3162)-SELECTED PROVISIONS

SECTION 1. SHORT TITLE AND TABLE OF CONTENTS.

(a) SHORT TITLE—This Act may be cited as the 'Uniting and Strengthening America by Providing Appropriate Tools Required to Intercept and Obstruct Terrorism (USA PATRIOT ACT) Act of 2001'.

ENHANCING DOMESTIC SECURITY AGAINST TERRORISM

SEC. 105. EXPANSION OF NATIONAL ELECTRONIC CRIME TASK FORCE INITIATIVE.

The Director of the United States Secret Service shall take appropriate actions to develop a national network of electronic crime task forces, based on the New York Electronic Crimes Task Force model, throughout the United States, for the purpose of preventing, detecting, and investigating various forms of electronic crimes, including potential terrorist attacks against critical infrastructure and financial payment systems.

TITLE II—ENHANCED SURVEILLANCE PROCEDURES

SEC. 201. AUTHORITY TO INTERCEPT WIRE, ORAL, AND ELECTRONIC COMMUNICATIONS RELATING TO TERRORISM.

Section 2516(1) of title 18, United States Code, is amended—

(1) by redesignating paragraph (p), as so redesignated by section 434(2) of the Antiterrorism and Effective Death Penalty Act of 1996 (Public Law 104-132; 110 Stat. 1274), as paragraph (r); and

(2) by inserting after paragraph (p), as so redesignated by section 201(3) of the Illegal Immigration Reform and Immigrant Responsibility

Act of 1996 (division C of Public Law 104-208; 110 Stat. 3009-565), the following new paragraph:

'(q) any criminal violation of section 229 (relating to chemical weapons); or sections 2332, 2332a, 2332b, 2332d, 2339A, or 2339B of this title (relating to terrorism); or'.

SEC. 202. AUTHORITY TO INTERCEPT WIRE, ORAL, AND ELECTRONIC COMMUNICATIONS RELATING TO COMPUTER FRAUD AND ABUSE OFFENSES.

Section 2516(1)(c) of title 18, United States Code, is amended by striking 'and section 1341 (relating to mail fraud),' and inserting 'section 1341 (relating to mail fraud), a felony violation of section 1030 (relating to computer fraud and abuse),'.

SEC. 203. AUTHORITY TO SHARE CRIMINAL INVESTIGATIVE INFORMATION.

(b) AUTHORITY TO SHARE ELECTRONIC, WIRE, AND ORAL INTERCEPTION INFORMATION—

(1) LAW ENFORCEMENT—Section 2517 of title 18, United States Code, is amended by inserting at the end the following:

'(6) Any investigative or law enforcement officer, or attorney for the Government, who by any means authorized by this chapter, has obtained knowledge of the contents of any wire, oral, or electronic communication, or evidence derived therefrom, may disclose such contents to any other Federal law enforcement, intelligence, protective, immigration, national defense, or national security official to the extent that such contents include foreign intelligence or counterintelligence (as defined in section 3 of the National Security Act of 1947 (50 U.S.C. 401a)), or foreign intelligence information (as defined in subsection (19) of section 2510 of this title), to assist the official who is to receive that information in the performance of his official duties. Any Federal official who receives information pursuant to this provision may use that information only as necessary in the conduct of that person's official duties subject to any limitations on the unauthorized disclosure of such information.'.

SEC. 204. CLARIFICATION OF INTELLIGENCE EXCEPTIONS FROM LIMITATIONS ON INTERCEPTION AND DISCLOSURE OF WIRE, ORAL, AND ELECTRONIC COMMUNICATIONS.

Section 2511(2)(f) of title 18, United States Code, is amended—

(1) by striking 'this chapter or chapter 121' and inserting 'this chapter or chapter 121 or 206 of this title'; and

(2) by striking 'wire and oral' and inserting 'wire, oral, and electronic'.

SEC. 209. SEIZURE OF VOICE-MAIL MESSAGES PURSUANT TO WARRANTS.

Title 18, United States Code, is amended—

(1) in section 2510—

(A) in paragraph (1), by striking beginning with 'and such' and all that follows through 'communication'; and

(B) in paragraph (14), by inserting 'wire or' after 'transmission of'; and

(2) in subsections (a) and (b) of section 2703—

(A) by striking 'CONTENTS OF ELECTRONIC' and inserting 'CONTENTS OF WIRE OR ELECTRONIC' each place it appears;

(B) by striking 'contents of an electronic' and inserting 'contents of a wire or electronic' each place it appears; and

(C) by striking 'any electronic' and inserting 'any wire or electronic' each place it appears.

SEC. 210. SCOPE OF SUBPOENAS FOR RECORDS OF ELECTRONIC COMMUNICATIONS.

Section 2703(c)(2) of title 18, United States Code, as redesignated by section 212, is amended—

(1) by striking 'entity the name, address, local and long distance telephone toll billing records, telephone number or other subscriber number or identity, and length of service of a subscriber' and inserting the following: 'entity the—

'(A) name;

'(B) address;

'(C) local and long distance telephone connection records, or records of session times and durations;

'(D) length of service (including start date) and types of service utilized;

'(E) telephone or instrument number or other subscriber number or identity, including any temporarily assigned network address; and

'(F) means and source of payment for such service (including any credit card or bank account number), of a subscriber'; and

(2) by striking 'and the types of services the subscriber or customer utilized,'.

SEC. 211. CLARIFICATION OF SCOPE.

Section 631 of the Communications Act of 1934 (47 U.S.C. 551) is amended—

(1) in subsection (c)(2)—

(A) in subparagraph (B), by striking 'or';

(B) in subparagraph (C), by striking the period at the end and inserting '; or'; and

(C) by inserting at the end the following:

'(D) to a government entity as authorized under chapters 119, 121, or 206 of title 18, United States Code, except that such disclosure shall not include records revealing cable subscriber selection of video programming from a cable operator.'; and

(2) in subsection (h), by striking 'A governmental entity' and inserting 'Except as provided in subsection (c)(2)(D), a governmental entity'.

SEC. 212. EMERGENCY DISCLOSURE OF ELECTRONIC COMMUNICATIONS TO PROTECT LIFE AND LIMB.

(a) DISCLOSURE OF CONTENTS—

(1) IN GENERAL—Section 2702 of title 18, United States Code, is amended—

(A) by striking the section heading and inserting the following:

'Sec. 2702. Voluntary disclosure of customer communications or records';

(B) in subsection (a)—

(i) in paragraph (2)(A), by striking 'and' at the end;

(ii) in paragraph (2)(B), by striking the period and inserting '; and'; and

(iii) by inserting after paragraph (2) the following:

'(3) a provider of remote computing service or electronic communication service to the public shall not knowingly divulge a record or other information pertaining to a subscriber to or customer of such service (not including the contents of communications covered by paragraph (1) or (2)) to any governmental entity.';

(C) in subsection (b), by striking 'EXCEPTIONS—A person or entity' and inserting 'EXCEPTIONS FOR DISCLOSURE OF COMMUNICATIONS—A provider described in subsection (a)';

(D) in subsection (b)(6)—

(i) in subparagraph (A)(ii), by striking 'or';

(ii) in subparagraph (B), by striking the period and inserting '; or'; and

(iii) by adding after subparagraph (B) the following:

'(C) if the provider reasonably believes that an emergency involving immediate danger of death or serious physical injury to any person requires disclosure of the information without delay.'; and

(E) by inserting after subsection (b) the following:

'(c) EXCEPTIONS FOR DISCLOSURE OF CUSTOMER RECORDS— A provider described in subsection (a) may divulge a record or other information pertaining to a subscriber to or customer of such service (not including the contents of communications covered by subsection (a)(1) or (a)(2))—

'(1) as otherwise authorized in section 2703;

'(2) with the lawful consent of the customer or subscriber;

'(3) as may be necessarily incident to the rendition of the service or to the protection of the rights or property of the provider of that service;

'(4) to a governmental entity if the provider reasonably believes that an emergency involving immediate danger of death or serious physical injury to any person justifies disclosure of the information; or

'(5) to any person other than a governmental entity.'.

(2) TECHNICAL AND CONFORMING AMENDMENT—The table of sections for chapter 121 of title 18, United States Code, is amended by striking the item relating to section 2702 and inserting the following:

'2702. Voluntary disclosure of customer communications or records.'.

(b) REQUIREMENTS FOR GOVERNMENT ACCESS—

(1) IN GENERAL—Section 2703 of title 18, United States Code, is amended—

(A) by striking the section heading and inserting the following:

'Sec. 2703. Required disclosure of customer communications or records';

(B) in subsection (c) by redesignating paragraph (2) as paragraph (3);

(C) in subsection (c)(1)—

(i) by striking '(A) Except as provided in subparagraph (B), a provider of electronic communication service or remote computing service may' and inserting 'A governmental entity may require a provider of electronic communication service or remote computing service to';

(ii) by striking 'covered by subsection (a) or (b) of this section) to any person other than a governmental entity.

'(B) A provider of electronic communication service or remote computing service shall disclose a record or other information pertaining to a subscriber to or customer of such service (not including the contents of communications covered by subsection (a) or (b) of this section) to a governmental entity' and inserting ')';

(iii) by redesignating subparagraph (C) as paragraph (2);

(iv) by redesignating clauses (i), (ii), (iii), and (iv) as subparagraphs (A), (B), (C), and (D), respectively;

(v) in subparagraph (D) (as redesignated) by striking the period and inserting '; or'; and

(vi) by inserting after subparagraph (D) (as redesignated) the following:

'(E) seeks information under paragraph (2).'; and

(D) in paragraph (2) (as redesignated) by striking 'subparagraph (B)' and insert 'paragraph (1)'.

(2) TECHNICAL AND CONFORMING AMENDMENT—The table of sections for chapter 121 of title 18, United States Code, is amended by striking the item relating to section 2703 and inserting the following:

'2703. Required disclosure of customer communications or records.'.

SEC. 213. AUTHORITY FOR DELAYING NOTICE OF THE EXECUTION OF A WARRANT.

Section 3103a of title 18, United States Code, is amended—

(1) by inserting '(a) IN GENERAL—' before 'In addition'; and

(2) by adding at the end the following:

'(b) DELAY—With respect to the issuance of any warrant or court order under this section, or any other rule of law, to search for and seize any property or material that constitutes evidence of a criminal offense in violation of the laws of the United States, any notice required, or that may be required, to be given may be delayed if—

'(1) the court finds reasonable cause to believe that providing immediate notification of the execution of the warrant may have an adverse result (as defined in section 2705);

'(2) the warrant prohibits the seizure of any tangible property, any wire or electronic communication (as defined in section 2510), or, except as expressly provided in chapter 121, any stored wire or electronic information, except where the court finds reasonable necessity for the seizure; and

'(3) the warrant provides for the giving of such notice within a reasonable period of its execution, which period may thereafter be extended by the court for good cause shown.'.

SEC. 217. INTERCEPTION OF COMPUTER TRESPASSER COMMUNICATIONS.

Chapter 119 of title 18, United States Code, is amended—

(1) in section 2510—

(A) in paragraph (18), by striking 'and' at the end;

(B) in paragraph (19), by striking the period and inserting a semicolon; and

(C) by inserting after paragraph (19) the following:

'(20) 'protected computer' has the meaning set forth in section 1030; and

'(21) 'computer trespasser'—

'(A) means a person who accesses a protected computer without authorization and thus has no reasonable expectation of privacy in any communication transmitted to, through, or from the protected computer; and

'(B) does not include a person known by the owner or operator of the protected computer to have an existing contractual relationship with the owner or operator of the protected computer for access to all or part of the protected computer.'; and

(2) in section 2511(2), by inserting at the end the following:

'(i) It shall not be unlawful under this chapter for a person acting under color of law to intercept the wire or electronic communications of a computer trespasser transmitted to, through, or from the protected computer, if—

'(I) the owner or operator of the protected computer authorizes the interception of the computer trespasser's communications on the protected computer;

'(II) the person acting under color of law is lawfully engaged in an investigation;

'(III) the person acting under color of law has reasonable grounds to believe that the contents of the computer trespasser's communications will be relevant to the investigation; and

'(IV) such interception does not acquire communications other than those transmitted to or from the computer trespasser.'.

SEC. 223. CIVIL LIABILITY FOR CERTAIN UNAUTHORIZED DISCLOSURES.

(a) Section 2520 of title 18, United States Code, is amended—

(1) in subsection (a), after 'entity', by inserting ', other than the United States,';

(2) by adding at the end the following:

'(f) ADMINISTRATIVE DISCIPLINE—If a court or appropriate department or agency determines that the United States or any of its departments or agencies has violated any provision of this chapter, and the court or appropriate department or agency finds that the circumstances surrounding the violation raise serious questions about whether or not an officer or employee of the United States acted willfully or intentionally with respect to the violation, the department or agency shall, upon receipt of a true and correct copy of the decision and findings of the court or appropriate department or agency promptly initiate a proceeding to determine whether disciplinary action against the officer or employee is warranted. If the head of the department or agency involved determines that disciplinary action is not warranted, he or she shall notify the Inspector General with jurisdiction over the department or agency concerned and shall provide the Inspector General with the reasons for such determination.'; and

(3) by adding a new subsection (g), as follows:

'(g) IMPROPER DISCLOSURE IS VIOLATION—Any willful disclosure or use by an investigative or law enforcement officer or governmental entity of information beyond the extent permitted by section 2517 is a violation of this chapter for purposes of section 2520(a).'.

APPENDIX 4:
SUMMARY OF FEDERAL AND STATE PRIVACY LAWS

SUMMARY OF FEDERAL PRIVACY LAWS[1]

The Administrative Procedure Act. (5 U.S.C. §§ 551, 554-558)

The Administrative Procedures Act establishes detailed procedures for Federal agencies to follow during administrative hearings. The Act's provisions prescribe, for example, the means by which agencies must notify individuals of their rights and liabilities, and how agencies may collect, present, and evaluate evidence and other data in such hearings.

The Cable Communications Policy Act (47 U.S.C. § 551)

The Cable Communications Policy Act requires cable television operators to inform their subscribers annually about the nature of personal data collected, data disclosure practices, and subscriber rights to inspect and correct errors in such data. The Act prohibits a cable television company from using the cable system to collect personal information about its subscribers without their prior consent, and generally bars the cable operator from disclosing such data. The Act authorizes damage awards of at least $1,000, and awards of punitive damages, costs, and attorneys' fees against cable television companies that violate the Act's subscriber privacy provisions.

The Census Confidentiality Statute (13 U.S.C. § 9)

The Census Confidentiality Statute prohibits any use of census data for other than the original statistical purpose. The statute also prohibits any disclosure of census data that would allow an individual to be identified, except to sworn officers and employees of the Census Bureau.

---

1   Source: The Better Business Bureau.

The Children's Online Privacy Protection Act of 1998 (15 U.S.C. §§ 6501 et seq., 16 C.F.R. § 312)

The Children's Online Privacy Protection Act of 1998 requires a website directed at children under 13 years of age to obtain "verifiable parental consent" before collecting personal information online from children. The COPPA regulation defines the term "collects" to encompass providing a child with the ability to have an e-mail account or the ability to post to a chat room, bulletin board, or other online forum. The COPPA also requires a covered Web site to disclose in a notice its online information collection and use practices with respect to children, and provide parents with the opportunity to review the personal information collected online from their children.

The Communications Assistance for Law Enforcement Statute (47 U.S.C. § 1001)

The Communications Assistance for Law Enforcement Statute reserves law enforcement's ability to engage in lawful electronic surveillance in the face of new technological developments. The statute increases the protections against governmental intrusions into the privacy of electronic communications and requires that the government obtain a court order before obtaining tracking information or location information about subscribers from mobile service providers, and explicitly states that it does not limit the rights of subscribers to use encryption.

The Computer Security Act (40 U.S.C. § 1441)

The Computer Security Act protects data maintained in government computers and requires each Federal agency to provide mandatory training in computer security awareness.

The Consumer Credit Reform Act of 1996

The Consumer Credit Reporting Reform Act of 1996 (Reform Act) overhauled the Fair Credit Reporting Act (below). The Reform Act requires more frequent and fuller notification to consumers, disclosure of all information, rather than only the substance of the information, in the consumer's file, and stricter reinvestigation when a consumer disputes the accuracy of information in his or her file. Imposes new restrictions on resellers of consumer credit reports and strengthens private enforcement rights for violations of the Fair Credit Reporting Act.

The Criminal Justice Information Systems Statute (42 U.S.C. § 3789g)

The Criminal Justice Information Systems Statute requires Federally-funded State and local criminal justice information systems to include information on the disposition of any arrest and permits individuals to see, copy, and correct information about themselves in the system.

The Customer Proprietary Network Information Statute (47 U.S.C. § 222)

The Customer Proprietary Network Information Statute restricts private sector access and use of customer data, and the disclosure of individualized customer data obtained for purposes of providing telecommunications service absent customer approval. The statute imposes restrictions on the use of such data in aggregate form.

The Driver's Privacy Protection Act (18 U.S.C. § 2721)

The Driver's Privacy Protection Act prohibits State Departments of Motor Vehicles (DMVs) from releasing "personal information" from drivers' licenses and motor vehicle registration records. Permits the release of the information to recipients who are using it for one or more specific statutory purposes, or where the subject of the record was furnished with an opportunity to limit the release of the information and did not do so. The Act penalizes the procurement of information from motor vehicle records for an unlawful purpose, or the making of a false representation to obtain such information from a DMV. The Act imposes a record keeping requirement on the resellers of such information. The Act does not interfere with the ability of states to enact laws furnishing greater privacy protection to their drivers and vehicle owners.

The Drug and Alcoholism Abuse Confidentiality Statute (21 U.S.C. § 1175; 42 U.S.C. § 290dd-3)

The Drug and Alcoholism Abuse Confidentiality Statute prohibit disclosure of information collected for federally-funded research and treatment of drug abuse and alcoholism. The statute also prohibits use of this information for any purpose outside of the research or treatment program, except in cases of medical emergency or where a court order has been issued. Such information is specifically protected from use against the subject of any criminal proceeding. Violators of the statute are subject to a fine.

The Electronic Communications Privacy Act (18 U.S.C. § 2701, et seq.)

The Electronic Communications Privacy Act prohibits persons from tampering with computers or accessing certain computerized records without authorization. The Act also prohibits providers of electronic communications services from disclosing the contents of stored communications. The Act usually requires that the customer be notified and given an opportunity to contest in court a government entity's request for access to electronic mail or other stored communications in the control of a provider of electronic communications services or remote computing services.

The Electronic Funds Transfer Act (15 U.S.C. § 1693, 1693m)

The Electronic Funds Transfer Act requires banks to make extensive disclosures to customers about specific electronic funds transfer (EFT) transactions, both at the time the transactions are made and in the form of periodic statements. The Act requires banks to notify customers, at the time they contract for EFT services, of their rights, liabilities, charges, procedures, etc., connected with the services, and of whom to contact if an unauthorized transfer is suspected. In the case of preauthorized periodic transfers—such as automatic bill paying—the bank must provide either positive or negative notice as to whether payments are being made on schedule. The Act mandates detailed procedures for the resolution of any inaccuracies in customer accounts, and imposes liability on the bank for errors in the transmission or documentation of transfers. An individual who prevails in a civil action for a violation of the Act may recover actual damages sustained, a penalty of $100 to $1,000, attorney's fees and court costs, and in limited situations, treble damages. Criminal penalties may be imposed for deliberate violations of the Act. Numerous federal agencies also have administrative responsibility for enforcing the provisions of this Act.

The Employee Polygraph Protection Act (29 U.S.C. § 2001, et seq.)

The Employee Polygraph Protection Act prohibits employers from requiring a polygraph test as a condition of employment or using the results of such tests as the sole basis for disciplining employees or taking other adverse employment actions. The Act bars employers from publicly disclosing the results of polygraph tests unless disclosure is made to the government pursuant to a court order or for the purpose of providing the government with information on criminal conduct. Employers that violate the Act may be subject to a fine of up to $10,000, injunctive relief such as employee reinstatements, and awards of damages, costs and attorneys' fees.

The Employee Retirement Income Security Act (29 U.S.C. § 1025)

The Employee Retirement Income Security Act requires employers to provide employees with access to information about their accrued retirement benefits.

The Equal Credit Opportunity Act (15 U.S.C. § 1691, et. seq.)

The Equal Credit Opportunity Act restricts inquiries into a credit applicant's sex, race, color, religion, or marital status. The Act prohibits the retention and preservation of certain information by creditors and requires the preservation of certain specified records relating to credit transactions. The Act regulates the manner in which information collected by creditors may be used in making decisions regarding the extension of credit. The Act requires that, when credit is denied or revoked, the applicant must be either notified of the reasons for the decision or informed of his right to learn the reasons. In suits brought for violations of the Equal Credit Opportunity Act, successful plaintiffs may recover actual damages, punitive damages, attorneys' fees and court costs. Individual or class action suits may be maintained for administrative, injunctive or declaratory relief. Numerous Federal agencies also have enforcement responsibility for the provisions of this Act.

The Equal Employment Opportunity Act (42 U.S.C. § 2000e, et seq.)

The Equal Employment Opportunity Act restricts collection and use of information that would result in employment discrimination on the basis of race, sex, religion, national origin and a variety of other characteristics.

The Fair Credit Billing Act (15 U.S.C. § 1666)

The Fair Credit Billing Act requires creditors, at the request of individual consumers, to investigate alleged billing errors and to provide documentary evidence of the individual's indebtedness. The Act prohibits creditors from taking action against individuals with respect to disputed debts while disputes are under investigation. Any creditor who fails to disclose required information is subject to a civil suit, with a minimum penalty of $100 and a maximum penalty of $1,000 on any individual credit transaction. The Act also imposes criminal liability on any person who knowingly and willfully gives false or inaccurate information, fails to disclose required information, or otherwise violates any requirement imposed by the Act. Any such person is subject to a fine of $5,000 and/or imprisonment for not more than one year.

The Fair Credit Reporting Act (15 U.S.C. § 1681 et seq.)

The Fair Credit Reporting Act regulates the collection and use of personal data by credit reporting agencies. The Act requires that when a data broker is hired to prepare an "investigative consumer report"—i.e., an investigation into the consumer's "character, general reputation, personal characteristics or mode of living" by means of interviews with friends, neighbors and associates—the request for information must be disclosed to the subject of the report, who is then entitled to learn the nature and scope of the inquiry requested. The Act requires that, if a consumer report is used in any decision to deny credit, insurance or employment, the report user must tell the consumer the name and address of the reporting agency. The Act prohibits disclosure of consumer reports maintained by consumer reporting agencies without consent unless such disclosure is made for a legitimate business purpose or pursuant to a court order. The Act requires reporting agencies to use procedures that will avoid reporting specified categories of obsolete information and to verify information in investigative consumer reports that are used more than once. The Act requires brokers to maintain security procedures, including procedures to verify the identity and stated purposes of recipients of consumer reports. Individuals may sue credit reporting agencies or parties who obtain consumer reports for violations of the Act. Individuals may recover for actual damages suffered, as well as attorneys' fees and court costs. Punitive damages or criminal penalties may also be imposed for willful violations of the Act. The Federal Trade Commission and other Federal agencies responsible for enforcing the provisions of this Act are also empowered to declare actions to be in violation of the applicable statute, issue cease and desist orders, and impose statutory penalties for noncompliance with agency orders.

The Fair Debt Collection Practices Act (15 U.S.C. § 1692 et seq.)

The Fair Debt Collection Practices Act limits the communications that debt collection agencies may make about the debtors whose accounts they are attempting to collect. The Act imposes liability on debt collectors for any actual damages sustained, as well as additional damages not to exceed $1,000, court costs and attorneys' fees. Numerous Federal agencies also have administrative responsibility for enforcing the provisions of this Act.

The Fair Housing Statute (42 U.S,C. §§ 3604, 3605)

The Fair Housing Statute restricts the collection and use of information that would result in housing discrimination on the basis of race, sex, religion, national origin and a variety of other factors.

The Family Educational Rights and Privacy Act (20 U.S.C. § 1232g)

The Family Educational Rights and Privacy Act permits a student or the parent of a minor student to inspect and challenge the accuracy and completeness of educational records which concern the student. The Act prohibits schools receiving public funds from using or disclosing the contents of a student's records without the consent of the student or of the parent of the minor student. The Act prohibits government access to personal data in educational records without a court order or lawfully issued subpoena, unless the government is seeking access to the records for a specified education-related purpose. The Act vests administrative enforcement in the Department of Education, and provides for termination of Federal funds if an institution violates the Act and compliance cannot be secured voluntarily.

The Freedom of Information Act (5 U.S.C. § 552) (FOIA)

Freedom of Information Act provides individuals with access to many types of records that are exempt from access under the Privacy Act, including many categories of personal information. Unlike those of the Privacy Act, FOIA procedures are available to non-resident foreign nationals.

The Gramm-Leach-Bliley Act (15 U.S.C. §§ 6801 et seq)

The Gramm-Leach-Bliley Act regulates the privacy of personally identifiable, nonpublic financial information disclosed to non-affiliated third parties by financial institutions. Requirements also attach to non-affiliated third parties to whom they transfer this information. The Act requires written or electronic notice of the categories of nonpublic personal information collected, categories of people to whom the information will be disclosed, consumer opt-out rights, and the company's confidentiality and security policies. The Act creates consumer right to opt out of disclosures to nonaffiliated parties before the disclosure occurs, subject to a long list of exceptions. The Act requires administrative, technical and physical safeguards to maintain the security, confidentiality, and integrity of the information. The Act generally prohibits disclosure of account numbers and access codes for credit, deposit or transaction accounts to a nonaffiliated party for marketing purposes.

The Health Insurance Portability and Accountability Act (Pub. Law No. 104-191 §§262,264: 45 C.F.R. §§160-164)

The Health Insurance Portability and Accountability Act is a Department of Health and Human Services regulation, which goes into effect in 2003, and applies to individually identifiable health information that has been maintained or transmitted by a covered entity. The Act applies directly to three types of entities: health plans, health care providers, and health care clearinghouses. The Act will also require these covered entities to apply many of its provisions to their business associates, including contractors, third-party administrators, researchers, life insurance issuers and employers. The Act requires health plans and health care providers to provide a written notice of how protected health information about an individual will be used, as well as an accounting of the circumstances surrounding certain disclosures of the information. The Act prohibits covered entities from disclosing covered information in a manner inconsistent with the notice. The Act-requires covered entities to obtain a patient's opt-in via "consent" form for both use and disclosure of protected information for treatment, payment or health care operations. The Act also requires covered entities to obtain a patient's more detailed opt in via an "authorization" form for both use and disclosure of protected information for purposes other than treatment, payment or health care operations. The Act permits several forms of marketing and fundraising uses of protected information subject to receipt of written consent and subsequent provision of opportunity to opt out. The Act requires patient authorization for transfers of protected information for routine marketing by third parties. The Act provides right to access, copy and amend the information in designated record sets, including in a business associate's records if not a duplicate of the information held by the provider or plan.

The Health Research Data Statute (42 U.S.C. § 242m)

The Health Research Data Statute prohibits disclosure of data collected by the National Centers for Health Services Research and for Health Statistics that would identify an individual in any way.

The Mail Privacy Statute (39 U.S.C. § 3623)

The Mail Privacy Statute prohibits opening of mail without a search warrant or the addressee's consent.

The Paperwork Reduction Act of 1980 (44 U.S.C. § 3501, et seq.)

The Paperwork Reduction Act prohibits an agency from collecting information from the public if another agency has already collected the same information, or if the Office of Management and Budget does not believe the agency either needs or can make use of the information. The Act requires each Federal data collection form to explain why the information is being collected, how it is to be used, and whether the individual's response is mandatory, required to obtain a benefit, or voluntary.

The Privacy Act (5 U.S.C. § 552a)

The Privacy Act mandates that personal data be collected as much as possible directly from the record subject. Generally prohibits collection of information about an individual's exercise of First Amendment rights (e.g., freedom of expression, assembly, and religion). The Act requires that when an agency requests information about an individual, it notify the individual of the agency's authorization and purpose for collecting information, the extra-agency disclosures ("routine uses") that may be made of the data collected, and the consequences to the individual for failing to provide the information. The Act requires agencies, on request, to provide individuals with access to records pertaining to them and an opportunity to correct or challenge the contents of the records. The Act restricts Federal agencies from disclosing personal data except for publicly announced purposes, and requires agencies to (1) keep an accounting of extra-agency disclosures; to (2) instruct record management personnel in the requirements of the Act and the rules for its implementation; and (3) "establish appropriate administrative, technical, and physical safeguards to insure the security and confidentiality of records." The Act places accountability for the handling of personal records on the record-keeping agency and its employees. The Act requires agencies to publish a detailed annual notice that describes each record system, the kind of information maintained, its sources, the policies governing management of the system, and the procedures for individuals to obtain access to records about themselves. The Act allows an individual harmed by a violation to sue the agency for an injunction, damages, and court costs. It also provides criminal penalties—fines of up to $5,000—against employees who disclose records in violation of the Act.

The Privacy Protection Act (42 U.S.C. § 2000aa)

The Privacy Protection Act prohibits government agents from conducting unannounced searches of press offices and files if no one in the press office is suspected of a crime. The Act requires instead that the government request voluntary cooperation or subpoena the material sought, giving the holder of the material a chance to contest the action in court. The Act directs the U.S. Attorney General to issue guidelines for seeking evidence from other non-suspect third parties, with special consideration to such traditionally confidential relationships as doctor-patient and priest-penitent.

The Right to Financial Privacy Act (12 U.S.C. § 3401, et seq.)

The Right to Financial Privacy Act requires Federal agencies seeking access to private financial records either: (1) to notify the subject of the purpose for which the records are sought and provide the subject with an opportunity to challenge the disclosure in court; or (2) to obtain a court order for direct access to the records if notice would allow the record subject to flee or destroy the evidence. The Act prohibits a Federal agency that has obtained access to an individual's financial records from disclosing the records to another agency without: (1) notifying the individual; and (2) obtaining certification from the receiving agency that the records are relevant to a legitimate law enforcement inquiry of the receiving agency. Where a government agency or a financial institution discloses records or information in violation of the Right to Financial Privacy Act, the agency or institution is liable to the customer for any actual damages sustained, a $100 penalty, punitive damages for willful or intentional violations, court costs, and attorney's fees.

The Tax Reform Act (26 U.S.C. §§ 6103, 6108, 7609)

The Tax Reform Act requires notice and opportunity—to challenge procedures (similar to those of the Right to Financial Privacy Act) before the Internal Revenue Service may obtain access to certain institutional records about an individual in the hands of certain private record keepers. The Act strictly limits disclosure of tax returns and return information, and in some cases requires a court order for disclosures to law enforcement agencies for purposes unrelated to tax administration.

The Telephone Consumer Protection Act (47 U.S.C. § 227)

The Telephone Consumer Protection Act requires entities who use the telephone to solicit individuals, to provide such individuals with the ability to prevent future telephone solicitations. The Act requires those who engage in telephone solicitations to maintain and honor lists of individuals who request not to receive such solicitations for ten years. The Act prohibits unsolicited commercial telephone calls using an artificial or pre-recorded voice without consumer consent, and prohibits the sending of unsolicited advertisements to facsimile machines.

The Video Privacy Protection Act (18 U.S.C. § 2710)

The Video Privacy Protection Act affords users and purchasers of commercial videotapes rights similar to those of patrons of libraries. The Act prohibits videotape sale or rental companies from disclosing customer names and addresses, and the subject matter of their purchases or rentals for direct marketing use, unless the customers have been notified of their right to prohibit such disclosures. The Act restricts videotape companies from disclosing personal data about customers without customers' consent or court approval. The Act requires that subscribers be notified and provided with an opportunity to contest a data request prior to a judicial determination. Video companies that violate the Video Privacy Protection Act may be liable for damage awards of at least $2500, punitive damages, costs and attorneys' fees.

Wiretap Statutes (18 U.S.C. § 2510, et seq.; 47 U.S.C. § 605)

Wiretap Statutes prohibit the use of eavesdropping technology and the interception of electronic mail, radio communications, data transmission and telephone calls without consent. The Federal Communications Commission also has a rule and tariff prescription prohibiting the recording of telephone conversations without notice or consent.

SUMMARY OF STATE PRIVACY LAWS

Bank Records Statutes

Bank records statutes prohibit financial institutions from disclosing financial records of a customer to a third party without legal process or customer consent.

Cable Television Statutes

Cable television statutes permit subscribers to correct information or have their names deleted from data files maintained by cable operators. These statutes prohibit disclosure of personal information collected by a cable operator unless the subscriber has had notice and has not objected to the disclosure.

Common Law Remedies

Common law remedies provide redress for invasion of privacy—i.e., intrusions into places or affairs as to which an individual has a reasonable expectation of privacy—public disclosure of privacy facts, defamation—i.e., disclosures of inaccurate personal information—and breach of duty of confidentiality. These remedies generally provide for money damages and, in some cases, nominal, special or punitive damages, and injunctive relief.

Computer Crime Statutes

Computer crime statutes prohibit individuals from tampering with computers or accessing certain computerized records without authorization. Persons engaged in such conduct are subject to criminal penalties, civil damages or both.

Credit Reporting Statutes

Credit reporting statutes prohibit collection by creditors of information on race, religion, or sex. These statutes also restrict disclosure by credit reporting agencies of credit information to third parties.

Criminal Justice Information Statutes

Criminal justice information statutes require law enforcement agencies to permit individuals to see, copy and correct information about themselves maintained in the criminal justice information systems. These statutes require that criminal justice information be reported promptly, completely and in standard format. These statues also have quality control requirements for computerized information systems and special requirements that arrest records indicate the disposition of the case. In addition, most of the State criminal justice information statutes require strict security measures to protect this information.

Employment Records Statutes

Employment records statutes prohibit employers from collecting information about a job applicant's race, sex, color, religion, national origin and other attributes. These statutes allow individuals access to personnel records held by their employers.

Fair Information Practices Statutes

Fair information practices statutes limit the type of information that State governments can collect and maintain about individuals. These statutes allow individuals to inspect and challenge information about them held by the State. They also restrict the ability of State governments to disclose personal data to third parties.

Genetic Information Statutes

Genetic information statutes limit use of genetic information for therapeutic or diagnostic purposes. These statutes prohibit use of information as a condition to determine eligibility for health, disability, life or other forms of insurance.

Insurance Records Statutes

Insurance records statutes require insurers to provide general information about their personal data practices to applicants and policyholders, with further information available upon request. These statutes require them to notify applicants about the collection and disclosure of personal data, and to specify when information is requested solely for marketing or research purposes. These statutes restrict the use of "pretext interviews," in which the identity or purpose of the interviewer is misrepresented, and require specific consent forms to be used for the collection of information that requires authorization from an individual. These statutes permit individuals who are denied insurance to learn the specific reasons for such denial and to obtain access to the information used in refusing coverage. Applicants or policy holders also may obtain access to non-privileged personal information about them, and may propose that such information be corrected, amended or deleted. Except where such disclosure is permitted by law, these statutes prohibit insurers from disclosing (without the individual's consent) information they collect on individuals.

Media Shield Statutes

Media shield statutes permit journalists to refuse to identify the sources of information received in the course of professional employment.

Medical Records Statutes

Medical records statutes allow individuals to have access to their medical records. These statutes limit the use and disclosure of medical or mental health records.

Polygraph Test Statutes

Polygraph test statutes restrict the use of mandatory polygraph tests as a condition for employment.

Privilege Statutes

Privilege statutes limit the introduction into legal proceedings of personal information maintained by professionals such as doctors, psychotherapists, attorneys, clergy and accountants, concerning individuals with whom they have a professional relationship.

School Records Statutes

School records statutes permit students and their parents to inspect and challenge the accuracy and completeness of school records. These statues limit the ability of schools to disclose information from school records to third parties.

Stored Wire Communications Statutes

Stored wire communications statutes require notice to subscribers before the government can access stored wire communications.

Tax Return Statutes

Tax Return Statutes prohibit disclosure by the government of State tax returns and return information.

Telephone/Facsimile Solicitation Statutes

Telephone/facsimile solicitation statutes restricts home telephone solicitations from using recorded messages; limits unsolicited fax advertisements.

The Uniform Commercial Code

The Uniform Commercial Code encourages financial institutions to disclose to their customers in a timely fashion the record of all transactions by holding the financial institution responsible for any errors until after the customer is informed of the bank's version of what has occurred.

Video Privacy Statutes

Video privacy statutes restrict videotape sales or rental companies from disclosing personal data about customers without their consent.

Wiretap Statutes

Wiretap statutes restrict electronic eavesdropping and interception of communications by wire or radio. Some states also have tariff prescriptions requiring common carriers operating within their jurisdictions to terminate subscribers who record telephone conversations without notice or consent.

APPENDIX 5:
INTERNET PRIVACY RESOURCE DIRECTORY

NAME	WEBSITE	FUNCTION	SERVICES
AMERICA LINKS UP	www.americalinksup.org	child online protection organization	public awareness and education campaign sponsored by a broad-based coalition of non-profit organizations, education groups, and corporations concerned with providing children with a safe and rewarding online experience.
AMERICAN CIVIL LIBERTIES UNION (ACLU)	www.aclu.org	advocacy organization	advocates individual rights by litigating, legislating, and educating the public on a broad array of issues affecting individual freedom in the United States; founding member of the Global Internet Liberty Campaign, an international coalition of organizations dedicated to protecting freedom of speech and the right to privacy in cyberspace.

NAME	WEBSITE	FUNCTION	SERVICES
ASSOCIATION FOR INTERACTIVE MEDIA (AIM)	www.interactivehq.org	trade organization	non-profit trade association for business users of the internet which includes companies that are committed to maximizing the value of the internet to businesses and consumers.
BETTER BUSINESS BUREAU (BBB)	www.bbb.org	business watch organization	operates an authenticated and verified "seal" program that helps consumers find reliable companies that pledge to meet tough advertising and dispute settlement standards, including responsible advertising to children.
CALL FOR ACTION	www.callforaction.org	consumer information hotline	international network of free consumer hotlines to assist consumer in resolving and mediating fraud and privacy disputes.
CENTER FOR DEMOCRACY AND TECHNOLOGY (CDT)	www.cdt.org	advocacy organization	works to promote democratic values and constitutional liberties in the digital age; seeks practical solutions to enhance free expression and privacy in global communications technologies; dedicated to building consensus among all parties interested in the future of the Internet and other new communications media; offers its "Operation Opt-Out," which allows users to easily generate form letters to be taken out of mailing lists.

NAME	WEBSITE	FUNCTION	SERVICES
CENTER FOR MEDIA EDUCATION	www.cme.org	child online protection organization	non-profit organization dedicated to improving the quality of electronic media, especially on behalf of children and families; involved in investigating the children's online marketplace.
RESOURCES FOR INTERNET PARENTS	www.netparents.org	child online protection organization	provides information on parental control software.
CHILDREN'S ADVERTISING REVIEW UNIT (CARU)	www.bbb.org/advertising/ childrensmonitor.asp	child online protection organization	first organization to develop self-regulatory guidelines for businesses advertising to children online; provides voluntary standards for the protection of children under the age of 12 including information on the disclosure of what information is being collected and its intended uses and the opportunity for the consumer to withhold consent for information collection for marketing purposes.
CONSUMER ACTION	www.consumer-action.org	advocacy organization	a non-profit, membership-based organization concerned with advancing consumer rights, referring consumers to complaint-handling agencies through its free hotline, publishing multilingual educational materials, and advocating for consumers in the media and before lawmakers.

NAME	WEBSITE	FUNCTION	SERVICES
CONSUMER PRIVACY GUIDE	www.consumerprivacyguide.org	information service	site offers extensive tips, a glossary of terms, and video tutorials with step-by-step instructions on how to take advantage of privacy settings for the programs you use online.
CPA WEBTRUST	www.cpawebtrust.org	online oversight organization	CPA firms that verify security systems of participating websites every 90 days and award icons of approval.
CYBERANGELS	www.cyberangels.org	child online protection organization	finds and reports illegal material online; educates families about online safety; works with schools and libraries; and shares basic internet tips and help resources.
DIRECT MARKETING ASSOCIATION (DMA)	www.the-dma.org	opting out service	Offers information on online marketing protections and advice on getting rid of unsolicited commercial e-mail; tells consumer how to delete their name from e-mail marketing lists and includes downloadable forms; peer review process acts on consumer complaints about DMA members and nonmembers.
ELECTRONIC FRONTIER FOUNDATION (EFF)	www.eff.org	advocacy organization	nonprofit organization working to guarantee that all civil liberties are protected on the Internet and in all digital communication arenas; provides a free telephone hotline for questions regarding legal rights and will answer your technical and legal questions via telephone, snail mail, and e-mail.

NAME	WEBSITE	FUNCTION	SERVICES
ELECTRONIC PRIVACY INFORMATION CENTER (EPIC)	www.epic.org	advocacy organization	nonprofit organization established to focus public attention on emerging civil liberties issues and to protect privacy and constitutional values.
EQUIFAX	www.equifax.com	credit reporting organization	one of the three major national credit reporting agencies where the consumer can order a copy of their credit report online; read fraud FAQs; and find out how to report credit card misuse or remove their name from pre-approved credit card offer mailing lists.
EXPERIAN	www.experian.com	credit reporting organization	one of the three major national credit reporting agencies where the consumer can order a copy of their credit report online; read fraud frequently asked questions and direct-mail marketing information; and find out how to report credit card misuse or remove their name from pre-approved credit card offer mailing lists.
FEDERAL TRADE COMMISSION (FTC)	www.ftc.gov	government organization	provides a wealth of information on current privacy legislation and related government news.
GETNETWISE	www.getnetwise.org	child online protection organization	resource for families and caregivers to help kids have safe, educational, and entertaining online experiences; includes a glossary of terms, a guide to online safety, directions for reporting online trouble, a directory of online safety tools, and a listing of great sites for kids to visit.

NAME	WEBSITE	FUNCTION	SERVICES
HUSH COMMUNICATIONS	www.hush.com	privacy enhancement technology organization	develops and distributes encryption technology to provide internet users with secure internet communications worldwide; allows users to protect the privacy of their email and Web site traffic.
INTERNET FRAUD WATCH	www.fraud.org	fraud and identity theft organization	provides tips, articles, bulletins, and other information on how to avoid fraud, protect your privacy, and safely surf the internet.
JUNKBUSTERS	www.junkbusters.com	junk mail oversight organization	site includes an array of information, resources and publication links as well as actionable tips and online tools to help the consumer eliminate junk e-mail, telemarketing calls, and other kinds of unwanted solicitations.
KIDZ PRIVACY SITE	www.ftc.gov/bcp/conline/edcams/ kidzprivacy/index.html	child online protection organization	FTC site which offers guidance to parents, children and website operators on the dos and don'ts of children's online privacy.
LUMERIA	www.lumeria.com	privacy enhancement technology organization	allows people to organize, securely access, and selectively share their information from any personal electronic device or computer that is connected to the net.
MAILSHELL	www.mailshell.com	junk mail oversight organization	offers advanced filtering technology against spam combined with more personalization, control, and privacy than any other service.

NAME	WEBSITE	FUNCTION	SERVICES
MEDIA AWARENESS NETWORK	www.media-awareness.ca	online resource for parents, educators, and youth	includes an interactive children's game on safe surfing.
NATIONAL FRAUD INFORMATION CENTER (NFIC)	www.fraud.org	advocacy organization	nationwide toll-free hotline for advice on telephone solicitations and how to report telemarketing fraud; provides tips, articles, bulletins, and other information on how to avoid fraud, protect your privacy, and safely surf the internet.
NATIONAL TELECOMMUNICATIONS AND INFORMATION ADMINISTRATION (NTIA)	www.ntia.doc.gov	government organization	primary source for domestic and international telecommunications and information technology issues including the federal Privacy Protection Acts; includes a listing of links to a range of privacy-related institutions and organizations.
NETCOALITION	www.netcoalition.com	trade organization	brings together many of the world's leading Internet companies and serves as a unified public policy voice on internet issues.
ONLINE PRIVACY ALLIANCE	www.privacyalliance.org	trade organization	a diverse group of corporations and associations who have come together to introduce and promote business-wide actions that create an environment of trust and foster the protection of individuals' privacy online.

NAME	WEBSITE	FUNCTION	SERVICES
ONLINE PUBLIC EDUCATION NETWORK (OPEN)	www.internetalliance.org/project-open/about.html	child online protection organization	offers information helpful for online novices, specific tips about parental empowerment and publishes guide entitled "Child Safety on the Information Highway."
OPERATION OPT-OUT	www.opt-out.cdt.org	opting out service	offers downloadable opt-out forms; links to companies that allow you to opt-out online.
PRIVACY RIGHTS CLEARINGHOUSE (PRC)	www.privacyrights.org	advocacy organization	provides in-depth information on a broad range of privacy issues.
PRIVACYX	www.privacyx.com	privacy enhancement technology organization	helps internet users take control of their online privacy; offers free anonymous encrypted email service that allows users to send and receive email with complete privacy and security.
PRIVASEEK	www.privaseek.com.	privacy enhancement technology organization	designs, builds, and manages systems and services that bring businesses and consumers together in a mutually beneficial permission-based environment; developed a control tool that enables consumers to automatically safeguard and gain value from the use of personal information; acts as a buffer between consumers and websites, allowing users to decide which information can be shared and allows consumer to store that information for safe and secure online use.

NAME	WEBSITE	FUNCTION	SERVICES
SPAMEX	www.spamex.com	junk mail oversight organization	disposable email address service allows users to identify the sources of spam mail and stop the non-permission use of their email addresses.
TRANS UNION CORPORATION	www.tuc.com	credit reporting organization	one of the three major national credit reporting agencies where the consumer can order a copy of their credit report online; read fraud FAQs; find out how to report credit card misuse or remove their name from pre-approved credit card offer mailing lists; find information on credit card scams, and the Marketing List Opt-Out section which tells how to delete one's name from junk mail lists.
TRUSTe	www.truste.org	online oversight organization	offers the latest advice and information about online privacy and awards seals to responsible websites that meet stringent privacy policy requirements and enforcement criteria.
U.S. CONSUMER GATEWAY	www.consumer.gov	government organization	provides a wide variety of federal information resources online; devoted to privacy and offers guidance on how to prohibit companies from using one's credit records for direct marketing and name from direct-mail and telemarketing lists.

NAME	WEBSITE	FUNCTION	SERVICES
WIRED KIDS	www.wiredkids.org	child online protection organization	official North American site of UNESCO's Innocence in Danger program; mission is to allow children to enjoy the vast benefits of the internet while at the same time protecting them from cybercriminals.
ZERO-KNOWLEDGE SYSTEMS	www.zeroknowledge.com	privacy enhancement technology organization	designs tools and strategies to protect the privacy of internet users; creates simple, easy-to-use software and services that integrate advanced mathematics, cryptography and source code.

Source: TRUSTe Organization

APPENDIX 6:
MICROSOFT CORPORATION COMPLAINT

012 3240

UNITED STATES OF AMERICA
FEDERAL TRADE COMMISSION

In the Matter of   )
)
MICROSOFT CORPORATION.   )   DOCKET NO. C-4069
        a corporation.   )
)

COMPLAINT

The Federal Trade Commission, having reason to believe that Microsoft, a corporation ("respondent") has violated the provisions of the Federal Trade Commission Act, and it appearing to the Commission that this proceeding is in the public interest, alleges:

1.   Respondent Microsoft is a Washington corporation with its principal office or place of business at One Microsoft Way, Redmond, Washington 98052. Respondent, a software and technology company, has advertised and promoted its sign-on and online wallet services, Passport and Passport Express Purchase (aka Passport Wallet), through the company's Web site at www.passport.com and elsewhere on the Internet.

2.   The acts and practices of respondent as alleged in this complaint have been in or affecting commerce, as "commerce" is defined in Section 4 of the Federal Trade Commission Act.

Passport Security

3.   Following the launch of Passport in October 1999, respondent disseminated or caused to be disseminated various versions of a "Microsoft .NET Passport Q&A" on Passport.com, including but not necessarily limited to that attached as Exhibit A, containing the following statements:

Security and Privacy

How secure is .NET Passport?

.NET Passport achieves a high level of Web Security by using technologies and systems designed to prevent unauthorized access to your personal information.

Exhibit A, Microsoft .NET Passport Q&A, http://www.passport.com/Consumer/ ConsumerQA.asp?lc.

4.   Respondent also disseminated or caused to be disseminated on the home page of its Web site at Passport.com various advertisements, including but not necessarily limited to that shown in Exhibit B, containing the following statements:

Security
Use .NET Passport from any computer on the Internet. Your .NET Passport is protected by powerful online security technology and a strict privacy policy.

Page 1 of 5

Exhibit B, Passport Home Page, http://www.passport.com/Consumer/Default.asp?lc=1033.

5.   Respondent also disseminated or caused to be disseminated various privacy policies on Passport.com, including but not limited to the attached Exhibit C, containing the following statements:

SECURITY OF YOUR PERSONAL INFORMATION

Your .NET Passport information is stored on secure .NET Passport servers that are protected in controlled facilities.

Exhibit C, Microsoft .NET Passport Privacy Policy, http://www.passport.com/Consumer/ PrivacyPolicy.asp?lc=1033.

6.   Through the means described in Paragraphs 3-5, respondent represented, expressly or by implication, that it maintained a high level of online security by employing sufficient measures reasonable and appropriate under the circumstances to maintain and protect the privacy and confidentiality of personal information obtained from or about consumers in connection with the Passport and Passport Wallet services.

7.   In truth and in fact, respondent did not maintain a high level of online security by employing sufficient measures reasonable and appropriate under the circumstances to maintain and protect the privacy and confidentiality of personal information obtained from or about consumers in connection with the Passport and Passport Wallet services. In particular, respondent failed to implement and document procedures that were reasonable and appropriate to: (1) prevent possible unauthorized access to the Passport system; (2) detect possible unauthorized access to the Passport system; (3) monitor the Passport system for potential vulnerabilities; and (4) record and retain system information sufficient to perform security audits and investigations. In light of these deficiencies, taken together, the representation set forth in Paragraph 6 was false or misleading.

Passport Wallet Security

8.   Respondent has promoted its Passport Express Purchase service, also referred to as Passport Wallet, as an online service that facilitates consumers' online purchases by transmitting credit card numbers, billing information, and shipping information stored in their Passport wallet to participating Express Purchase sites.

9.   Following the launch of Passport Wallet in October 1999, respondent disseminated or caused to be disseminated on the home page of its Web site at Passport.com various advertisements, including but not necessarily limited to that shown in Exhibit B, containing the following statements:

Store information in .NET Passport wallet that will help you make faster safer online purchases at any .NET Passport express purchase site.

Exhibit B, Passport Home Page, http://www.passport.com/Consumer/Default.asp?lc=1033.

10.   Respondent also disseminated or caused to be disseminated various versions of a "Microsoft .NET Passport Q&A" on Passport.com, including but not necessarily limited to that attached as Exhibit A, containing the following statements:

What is Microsoft .NET Passport and what can I do with it?

. . .

With a .NET Passport, you can:

. . .

Make faster, more secure online purchases with .NET Passport express purchase.

Exhibit A, Microsoft .NET Passport Q&A, http://www.passport.com/Consumer/ ConsumerQA.asp?lc.

11.   Through the means described in paragraphs 9 and 10, respondent represented, expressly or by implication, that purchases made at a Passport Express Purchase site with Passport Wallet are safer or more secure than purchases made at the same Passport Express Purchase site without using the Passport Wallet.

12.   In truth and in fact, purchases made at a Passport Express Purchase site with Passport Wallet are not, for most consumers, safer or more secure than purchases made at the same Passport Express Purchase site without using the Passport Wallet. Most consumers making credit card purchases at a Passport Express Purchase site receive identical security whether they use Passport Wallet to complete a transaction or purchase directly from the Passport Express Purchase site without using a Passport Wallet. Therefore, the representations set forth in paragraph 11 were false or misleading.

Passport Privacy - Data Collection

13.   Respondent has disseminated or caused to be disseminated various privacy policies on Passport.com, including but not limited to the attached Exhibit C, which contains the following statements:

This Privacy Statement discloses the privacy practices for the .NET Passport Web Site and .NET Passport Services in accordance with the requirements of the TRUSTe Privacy Program. When you visit a web site displaying the TRUSTe trademark, you can expect to be notified of [w]hat personally identifiable information of yours is collected. . . .

Exhibit C, Microsoft .NET Passport Privacy Policy, http://www.passport.com/Consumer/ PrivacyPolicy.asp?lc=1033.

14.   This privacy statement also described in detail the information collected from or about consumers in connection with their use of the Passport, including, but not limited to: what information is collected by Passport when a consumer registers at the Passport.com site; what information is collected by Passport and by a participating site when a consumer registers for Passport through that participating site; what information is collected by participating sites when a consumer signs in with a Passport; "operational" information generated in connection with a Passport account; the association of a unique identification number with every Passport account; and the collection of sign-in and other information in temporary cookies that are deleted when the consumer signs out of Passport.

15.   Through the means described in paragraphs 13-14, respondent represented, expressly or by implication, that Passport did not collect any personally identifiable information other than that described in its privacy policy.

16.   In truth and in fact, Passport did collect personally identifiable information other than that described in its privacy policy. In particular, Passport collected, and maintained for a limited period of time, a personally

Page 3 of 5

identifiable record of the sites to which a Passport user signed in, along with the dates and times of sign in, which customer service representatives linked to a user's name in order to respond to a user's request for service. Therefore, the representation set forth in paragraph 15 was false or misleading.

<u>Kids Passport</u>

17.   Respondent has promoted its Kids Passport service as an online service that assists parents in protecting their children's online privacy.

18.   Since the introduction of Kids Passport in April 2000, respondent has disseminated or caused to be disseminated various Kids Passport web pages and privacy policies, including but not necessarily limited to the attached Exhibits D and E, which contain the following statements:

A.   Welcome to Kids Passport
       Helping parents protect their children's privacy online

       . . .

       Learn about the Children's Online Privacy Protection Act
       Discover how Passport Kids is helping parents to keep their children's identity safe online.
       . . .

       Microsoft Kids Passport is a free service that helps you conveniently protect and control your children's online privacy. . . With Kids Passport, you can grant or deny consent to participation (sic) web sites (including the Microsoft family of web sites) to collect personal information from your children. In addition, you can make specific choices for each child and for each site, all in one convenient, centralized location.

Exhibit D. Kids Passport web pages, http://kids.passport.com.

B.   Microsoft Kids Passport Privacy Statement

       Microsoft is especially concerned about the safety and protection of children's personal information collected and used online. Microsoft Kids Passport ("Kids Passport") allows parents to consent to the collection, use and sharing of their children's information with Passport participating sites and services that have agreed to use Kids Passport as their parental consent process.

       . . .

       USE OF CHILDREN'S PERSONAL INFORMATION BY PASSPORT

       . . .

       Passport does not share this information contained in your child's Passport profile with third parties. except for Passport participating sites where you have consented to such sharing, or as otherwise disclosed in this statement.

       . . .

       CONTROL OF CHILDREN'S PERSONAL INFORMATION
       Kids Passport allow you to limit the amount of information shared with the sites and services participating in the Kids Passport program. You can choose to allow Passport to share all of the information in your child's Passport profile with a participating site or service, or you can limit the information shared to just a unique identifier or age range.
       . . .

Page 4 of 5

Exhibit E, Microsoft Kids Passport Privacy Statement, http://www.passport.com/
consumer/privacy/policy.asp/PPlcid=1033.

19.   Through the means described in Paragraph 18, respondent represented, expressly or by implication,
that the Kids Passport service provided parents with control over the information their children could provide to
participating Passport sites and the use of that information by such sites.

20.   In truth and in fact, the Kids Passport service did not provide parents with control over the information
their children could provide to participating Passport sites and the use of that information by such sites. For
instance, once a parent set up a child's Passport account and provided consent for the collection and/or
disclosure of the types of personal information listed in respondent's privacy policy, respondent permitted the
child to edit or change certain fields of personal information and change account settings set by the parent.
Respondent also failed to clearly inform parents that in some instances information would be disclosed to
Passport Web sites that do not participate in the Kids Passport service.   Therefore, the representations set
forth in paragraph 19 were false or misleading.

21.   The acts and practices of respondent as alleged in this complaint constituted unfair or deceptive acts
or practices in or affecting commerce in violation of Section 5(a) of the Federal Trade Commission Act.

THEREFORE, the Federal Trade Commission this twentieth day of December, 2002, has issued this complaint
against respondent.

By the Commission.

Donald S. Clark
Secretary

Page 5 of 5

APPENDIX 7:
MICROSOFT CORPORATION CONSENT ORDER

UNITED STATES OF AMERICA
FEDERAL TRADE COMMISSION

In the Matter of	)	FILE NO. 012 3240
	)	
MICROSOFT CORPORATION,	)	AGREEMENT CONTAINING
a corporation.	)	CONSENT ORDER
	)	

The Federal Trade Commission has conducted an investigation of certain acts and practices of Microsoft, a corporation ("proposed respondent"). Proposed respondent, having been represented by counsel, is willing to enter into an agreement containing a consent order resolving the allegations contained in the attached draft complaint. Therefore,

IT IS HEREBY AGREED by and between Microsoft, by its duly authorized officer, and counsel for the Federal Trade Commission that:

1. Proposed respondent Microsoft is a Washington corporation with its principal office or place of business at One Microsoft Way, Redmond, Washington 98052.

2. Proposed respondent admits all the jurisdictional facts set forth in the draft complaint.

3. Proposed respondent waives:

   (a) Any further procedural steps;

   (b) The requirement that the Commission's decision contain a statement of findings of fact and conclusions of law; and

   (c) All rights to seek judicial review or otherwise to challenge or contest the validity of the order entered pursuant to this agreement.

4. This agreement shall not become part of the public record of the proceeding unless and until it is accepted by the Commission. If this agreement is accepted by the Commission, it, together with the

Page 1 of 8

draft complaint, will be placed on the public record for a period of thirty (30) days and information about it publicly released. The Commission thereafter may either withdraw its acceptance of this agreement and so notify proposed respondent, in which event it will take such action as it may consider appropriate, or issue and serve its complaint (in such form as the circumstances may require) and decision in disposition of the proceeding.

5.   This agreement is for settlement purposes only and does not constitute an admission by proposed respondent that the law has been violated as alleged in the draft complaint, or that the facts as alleged in the draft complaint, other than the jurisdictional facts, are true.

6.   This agreement contemplates that, if it is accepted by the Commission, and if such acceptance is not subsequently withdrawn by the Commission pursuant to the provisions of Section 2.34 of the Commission's Rules, the Commission may, without further notice to proposed respondent, (1) issue its complaint corresponding in form and substance with the attached draft complaint and its decision containing the following order in disposition of the proceeding, and (2) make information about it public. When so entered, the order shall have the same force and effect and may be altered, modified, or set aside in the same manner and within the same time provided by statute for other orders. The order shall become final upon service. Delivery of the complaint and the decision and order to proposed respondent's address as stated in this agreement by any means specified in Section 4.4(a) of the Commission's Rules shall constitute service. Proposed respondent waives any right it may have to any other manner of service. The complaint may be used in construing the terms of the order. No agreement, understanding, representation, or interpretation not contained in the order or the agreement may be used to vary or contradict the terms of the order.

7.   Proposed respondent has read the draft complaint and consent order. It understands that it may be liable for civil penalties in the amount provided by law and other appropriate relief for each violation of the order after it becomes final.

ORDER

DEFINITIONS

For purposes of this order, the following definitions shall apply:

1.   "Personally identifiable information" or "personal information" shall mean individually identifiable information from or about an individual including, but not limited to: (a) a first and last name; (b) a home or other physical address, including street name and name of city or town; (c) an email address or other online contact information, such as an instant messaging user identifier or a screen name that reveals an

Page 2 of 8

individual's email address; (d) a telephone number; (e) a Social Security Number; (f) a persistent identifier, such as a customer number held in a "cookie" or processor serial number, that is combined with other available data that identifies an individual; or (g) any information that is combined with any of (a) through (f) above.

2.   "Covered online service" shall mean Passport, Kids Passport, Passport Wallet, any substantially similar product or service, or any multisite online authentication service.

3.   Unless otherwise specified, "respondent" shall mean Microsoft Corporation, its successors and assigns and its officers, agents, representatives, and employees acting within the scope of their authority on behalf of, or in active concert or participation with Microsoft Corporation.

4.   "Commerce" shall mean as defined in Section 4 of the Federal Trade Commission Act, 15 U.S.C. § 44.

I.

IT IS ORDERED that respondent, directly or through any corporation, subsidiary, division, or other device, in connection with the advertising, marketing, promotion, offering for sale, or sale of a covered online service, in or affecting commerce, shall not misrepresent in any manner, expressly or by implication, its information practices, including:

A.   what personal information is collected from or about consumers;

B.   the extent to which respondent's product or service will maintain, protect or enhance the privacy, confidentiality, or security of any personally identifiable information collected from or about consumers;

C.   the steps respondent will take with respect to personal information it has collected in the event that it changes the terms of the privacy policy in effect at the time the information was collected;

D.   the extent to which the service allows parents to control what information their children can provide to participating sites or the use of that information by such sites; and

E.   any other matter regarding the collection, use, or disclosure of personally identifiable information.

Page 3 of 8

II.

IT IS FURTHER ORDERED that respondent, and its successors and assigns, in connection with the advertising, marketing, promotion, offering for sale, or sale of a covered online service, in or affecting commerce, shall establish and maintain a comprehensive information security program in writing that is reasonably designed to protect the security, confidentiality, and integrity of personal information collected from or about consumers. Such program shall contain administrative, technical, and physical safeguards appropriate to respondent's size and complexity, the nature and scope of respondent's activities, and the sensitivity of the personal information collected from or about consumers, including:

A. The designation of an employee or employees to coordinate and be accountable for the information security program.

B. The identification of material internal and external risks to the security, confidentiality, and integrity of customer information that could result in the unauthorized disclosure, misuse, alteration, destruction, or other compromise of such information, and assessment of the sufficiency of any safeguards in place to control these risks. At a minimum, this risk assessment should include consideration of risks in each area of relevant operation, including: (1) employee training and management; (2) information systems, including network and software design, information processing, storage, transmission and disposal; and (3) prevention, detection, and response to attacks, intrusions, or other systems failures.

C. Design and implementation of reasonable safeguards to control the risks identified through risk assessment, and regular testing or monitoring of the effectiveness of the safeguards' key controls, systems, and procedures.

D. Evaluation and adjustment of respondent's information security program in light of the results of the testing and monitoring required by paragraph C, any material changes to respondent's operations or business arrangements, or any other circumstances that respondent knows or has reason to know may have a material impact on its information security program.

III.

Page 4 of 8

IT IS FURTHER ORDERED that respondent obtain within one (1) year, and on a biannual basis thereafter, an assessment and report from a qualified, objective, independent third-party professional, using procedures and standards generally accepted in the profession, that certifies:

A.   that respondent has in place a security program that provides protections that meet or exceed the protections required by Part II of this order; and

B.   that respondent's security program is operating with sufficient effectiveness to provide reasonable assurance that the security, confidentiality, and integrity of consumer's personal information has been protected.

The report required by this paragraph shall be prepared by a Certified Information System Security Professional (CISSP) or by a person or organization approved by the Associate Director for Enforcement, Bureau of Consumer Protection, Federal Trade Commission.

IV.

IT IS FURTHER ORDERED that respondent, and its successors and assigns, shall for a period of five (5) years after the date of service of this order maintain and upon request make available to the Federal Trade Commission for inspection and copying a print or electronic copy of the following documents relating to compliance with this order:

A.   a sample copy of each different print, broadcast, cable, or Internet advertisement, promotion, information collection form, Web page, screen, email message, or other document containing any representation to consumers regarding respondent's collection, use, and security of personal information from or about consumers. Each Web page copy shall be dated and contain the full URL of the Web page where the material was posted online. Electronic copies shall include all text and graphics files, audio scripts, and other computer files used in presenting the information on the Web. Provided, however, that after creation of any Web page or screen in compliance with this order, respondent shall not be required to retain a print or electronic copy of any amended Web page or screen to the extent that the amendment does not affect respondent's compliance obligations under this order;

B.   all plans, reports, studies, reviews, audits, audit trails, policies, and training materials, whether prepared by or on behalf of respondent, relating to respondent's compliance with this order; and

Page 5 of 8

C.   any documents, whether prepared by or on behalf of respondent, that contradict, qualify, or call into question respondent's compliance with this order.

V.

IT IS FURTHER ORDERED that respondent, and its successors and assigns, shall deliver a copy of this order to all current and future principals, officers, directors, and managers, and to all current and future employees, agents, and representatives having managerial responsibilities relating to the subject matter of this order. Respondent shall deliver this order to such current personnel within thirty (30) days after the date of service of this order, and to such future personnel within thirty (30) days after the person assumes such position or responsibilities.

VI.

IT IS FURTHER ORDERED that respondent Microsoft Corporation, and its successors and assigns, shall notify the Commission at least thirty (30) days prior to any change in the corporation that may affect compliance obligations arising under this order, including, but not limited to, a dissolution, assignment, sale, merger, or other action that would result in the emergence of a successor corporation; the creation or dissolution of a subsidiary, parent, or affiliate that engages in any acts or practices subject to this order; the proposed filing of a bankruptcy petition; or a change in the corporate name or address. Provided, however, that, with respect to any proposed change in the corporation about which respondent learns less than thirty (30) days prior to the date such action is to take place, respondent shall notify the Commission as soon as is practicable after obtaining such knowledge. All notices required by this Part shall be sent by certified mail to the Associate Director, Division of Enforcement, Bureau of Consumer Protection, Federal Trade Commission, Washington, D.C. 20580.

VII.

IT IS FURTHER ORDERED that respondent Microsoft Corporation, and its successors and assigns, shall within sixty (60) days after service of this order, and at such other times as the Federal Trade Commission may require, file with the Commission a report, in writing, setting forth in detail the manner and form in which they have complied with this order.

Page 6 of 8

VIII.

This order will terminate twenty (20) years from the date of its issuance, or twenty (20) years from the most recent date that the United States or the Federal Trade Commission files a complaint (with or without an accompanying consent decree) in federal court alleging any violation of the order, whichever comes later; provided, however, that the filing of such a complaint will not affect the duration of:

A.   Any Part in this order that terminates in less than twenty (20) years;

B.   This order's application to any respondent that is not named as a defendant in such complaint; and

C.   This order if such complaint is filed after the order has terminated pursuant to this Part.

Provided, further, that if such complaint is dismissed or a federal court rules that the respondent did not violate any provision of the order, and the dismissal or ruling is either not appealed or upheld on appeal, then the order will terminate according to this Part as though the complaint had never been filed, except that the order will not terminate between the date such complaint is filed and the later of the deadline for appealing such dismissal or ruling and the date such dismissal or ruling is upheld on appeal.

Signed this _____ day of _____, 2002.

MICROSOFT CORPORATION

By: _____

BRADFORD SMITH
Senior Vice President

_____

CHARLES F. BUFFON
Covington & Burling
Counsel for Respondent Microsoft Corporation

FEDERAL TRADE COMMISSION

Page 7 of 8

ELLEN R. FINN
Counsel for the Federal Trade Commission

APPROVED:

JESSICA RICH
Assistant Director
Division of Financial Practices

J. HOWARD BEALES, III
Director
Bureau of Consumer Protection

Page 8 of 8

APPENDIX 8:
LIBERTY FINANCIAL COMPLAINT

UNITED STATES OF AMERICA
FEDERAL TRADE COMMISSION

In the Matter of)	
)	
LIBERTY FINANCIAL COMPANIES, INC.)	DOCKET NO. C-3891
a corporation.)	
)	
)	

COMPLAINT

The Federal Trade Commission, having reason to believe that Liberty Financial Companies, Inc., a corporation ("respondent"), has violated the provisions of the Federal Trade Commission Act, and it appearing to the Commission that this proceeding is in the public interest, alleges:

1.   Respondent Liberty Financial Companies, Inc., is a Massachusetts corporation with its principal office or place of business at 600 Atlantic Avenue, Boston, Massachusetts 02210.

2.   Respondent has operated a World Wide Web ("Web") site located at *http://www.younginvestor.com* (the "Website").

3.   The acts and practices of respondent alleged in this complaint have been in or affecting commerce, as "commerce" is defined in Section 4 of the Federal Trade Commission Act.

4.   Respondent has disseminated or caused to be disseminated on its Website certain Web pages directed at children known as The Young Investor Measure Up Survey area. [*Exhibit A*]. At this area, respondent conducts a survey that collects from participants numerous items of information such as the individual's: weekly amount of allowance; types of financial gifts received such as stocks, bonds and mutual funds, and from whom; spending habits; part time work history; plans for college; and family finances including ownership of any mutual funds or investments in the Stein Roe Young Investor Fund offered by respondent. The survey states that "[a]ll of your answers will be totally anonymous." The survey ends with a section entitled "Entry Form" that asks participants what prize they would prefer if they win the "quarterly drawing," and asks if they "would like to be added to the Young Investor e-mail newsletter." The survey collects personal identifying information, including name, age, and gender, and participants in the survey are also told to provide e-mail address and street address in order to

Page 1 of 3

receive the newsletter and for identification purposes if they win the drawing.

5.   Through the means described in Paragraph 4, respondent has represented, expressly or by implication, that it maintains the information it collects at the Measure Up Survey area in an anonymous manner.

6.   In truth and in fact, respondent does not maintain the information it collects at the Measure Up Survey area in an anonymous manner because individuals can be identified with their responses to the survey. While respondent has not sold, rented, or otherwise marketed the information to any third party, respondent compiles and maintains a database that combines the personal identifying information that it collects in the Entry Form section of the survey, including name, address, and e-mail address, with all other survey responses. Therefore, the representation set forth in Paragraph 5 was, and is, false or misleading.

7.   The Measure Up Survey [*Exhibit A*] contains the following statements:

A.   "Would you like to be added to the Young Investor e-mail newsletter?"

B.   "Each Quarter, one participant will win his or her choice of a digital video camera, CD ROM drive or flatbed scanner."

C.   "If you are chosen as a winner in the quarterly drawing, which prize would you like?

  ○ Connectix color digital video camera
  ○ CD ROM drive
  ○ Flatbed scanner"

The survey then requests personal identifying information from the participants, including name, residence, and e-mail address, and states that this information "[m]ust be completed to get our newsletter" and "will only be used to contact you if you win."

8.   Through the means described in Paragraph 7, respondent has represented, expressly or by implication, that:

A.   Participants in the Measure Up Survey who submit the requested personal identifying information receive upon request respondent's Young Investor e-mail newsletter.

B.   In each quarter, a participant in the Measure Up Survey who submits the requested personal identifying information is selected to win his or her choice of specified prizes.

Page 2 of 3

9.   In truth and in fact:

      A.   Participants in the Measure Up Survey who submit the requested personal identifying information do not receive upon request respondent's Young Investor e-mail newsletter. Respondent has not provided an e-mail newsletter to any of the participants in the survey and, in fact, has never developed such an e-mail newsletter.

      B.   A participant in the Measure Up Survey who submits the requested personal identifying information has not been selected in each quarter to win his or her choice of specified prizes.

Therefore, the representations set forth in Paragraph 8 were, and are, false or misleading.

10.   The acts and practices of respondent as alleged in this complaint constitute unfair or deceptive acts or practices in or affecting commerce in violation of Section 5(a) of the Federal Trade Commission Act.

      THEREFORE, the Federal Trade Commission this twelfth day of August, 1999, has issued this complaint against respondent.

      By the Commission.

                         Benjamin I. Berman
                         Acting Secretary

Page 3 of 3

APPENDIX 9:
LIBERTY FINANCIAL CONSENT ORDER

UNITED STATES OF AMERICA

FEDERAL TRADE COMMISSION

In the Matter of

LIBERTY FINANCIAL COMPANIES, INC., a corporation.

FILE NO. 982 3522

AGREEMENT CONTAINING CONSENT ORDER

The Federal Trade Commission has conducted an investigation of certain acts and practices of Liberty Financial Companies, Inc., a corporation ("proposed respondent"). Proposed respondent, having been represented by counsel, is willing to enter into an agreement containing a consent order resolving the allegations contained in the attached draft complaint. Therefore,

IT IS HEREBY AGREED by and between Liberty Financial Companies, Inc., by its duly authorized officer, and counsel for the Federal Trade Commission that:

1. Proposed respondent Liberty Financial Companies, Inc. is a Massachusetts corporation with its principal office or place of business at 600 Atlantic Avenue, Boston, Massachusetts 02210.

2. Proposed respondent admits all the jurisdictional facts set forth in the draft complaint.

3. Proposed respondent waives:

(a) Any further procedural steps;

(b) The requirement that the Commission's decision contain a statement of findings of fact and conclusions of law; and

(c) All rights to seek judicial review or otherwise to challenge or contest the validity of the order entered pursuant to this agreement.

4. This agreement shall not become part of the public record of the proceeding unless and until it is accepted by the Commission. If this agreement is accepted by the Commission, it, together with the draft complaint, will be placed on the public record for a period of sixty (60) days and information about it publicly released. The Commission thereafter may either withdraw its acceptance of this agreement and so notify proposed respondent, in which event it will take such action as it may consider appropriate, or issue and serve its complaint (in such form as the circumstances may require) and decision in disposition of the proceeding.

5. This agreement is for settlement purposes only and does not constitute an admission by proposed respondent that the law has been violated as alleged in the draft complaint, or that the facts as alleged in the draft complaint, other than the jurisdictional facts, are true.

6. This agreement contemplates that, if it is accepted by the Commission, and if such acceptance is not subsequently withdrawn by the Commission pursuant to the provisions of Section 2.34 of the Commission's Rules, the Commission may, without further notice to proposed respondent, (1) issue its complaint corresponding in form and substance with the attached draft complaint and its decision containing the following order in disposition of the proceeding, and (2) make information about it public. When so entered, the order shall have the same force and effect and may be altered, modified, or set aside in the same manner and within the same time provided by statute for other orders. The order shall become final upon service. Delivery of the complaint and the decision and order to proposed respondent's address as stated in this agreement by any means specified in Section 4.4(a) of the Commission's Rules shall constitute service. Proposed respondent waives any right it may have to any other manner of service. The complaint may be used in construing the terms of the order. No agreement, understanding, representation, or interpretation not contained in the order or the agreement may be used to vary or contradict the terms of the order.

7. Proposed respondent has read the draft complaint and consent order. It understands that it may be liable for civil penalties in the amount provided by law and other appropriate relief for each violation of the order after it becomes final.

ORDER DEFINITIONS

For purposes of this order, the following definitions shall apply:

1. "Child" or "children" shall mean an individual under the age of thirteen (13).

2. "Parents" or "parental" shall mean a legal guardian, including, but not limited to, a biological or adoptive parent.

3. "Personal information" shall mean individually identifiable information about an individual collected online, including first and last name, home or other physical address including street name and name of a city or town, e-mail address, telephone number, Social Security number, or any information concerning the child or the parents of that child that the website collects online from the child and combines with an identifier described in this definition.

4. "Disclosure" shall mean, with respect to personal information, (a) the release of personal information collected from a child in identifiable form for any purpose, except where such information is provided to a person other than respondent who provides support for the internal operations of the website and does not disclose or use that information for any other purpose, and (b) making personal information collected from a child by a website directed to children or at any commercial website where respondent has actual knowledge that it is collecting personal information from a child, publicly available in identifiable form, by any means including, but not limited to, public posting through the Internet, or through a home page of a website, a pen pal service, an electronic mail service, a message board, or a chat room.

5. "Clear(ly) and prominent(ly)" shall mean in a type size and location that are not obscured by any distracting elements and are sufficiently noticeable for an ordinary consumer to read and comprehend, and in a typeface that contrasts with the background against which it appears.

6. "Electronically verifiable signature" shall mean a digital signature or other electronic means that ensures a valid consent by requiring: (1) authentication (guarantee that the message has come from the person who claims to have sent it); (2) integrity (proof that the message contents have not been altered, deliberately or accidentally, during transmission); and (3) non-repudiation (certainty that the sender of the message cannot later deny sending it).

7. "Verifiable parental consent" shall mean obtaining consent by any reasonable effort (taking into consideration available technology), including a request for authorization for future collection, use, and disclosure described in the notice, to ensure that a parent of a child re-

ceives notice of the respondent's personal information collection, use, and disclosure practices, and authorizes the collection, use, and disclosure, as applicable, of personal information and the subsequent use of that information before that information is collected from that child. Such reasonable efforts may include any of the following means: (1) a signed statement transmitted by postal mail or facsimile; (2) authorizing a charge to a credit card via a secure server; (3) e-mail accompanied by an electronically verifiable signature; (4) a procedure that is specifically authorized by statute, regulation, or guide issued by the Commission; or (5) such other procedure that ensures verified parental consent and ensures the identity of the parent, such as the use of a reliable certifying authority.

8. "Website directed to children" shall mean a commercial website targeted to children, or that portion of a commercial website that is targeted to children. Provided however, that a commercial website or a portion of a commercial website shall not be deemed directed to children solely for referring or linking to a commercial website directed to children by using information location tools, including a directory, index, reference, pointer, or hypertext link.

9. Unless otherwise specified, "respondent" shall mean Liberty Financial Companies, Inc., its successors and assigns and its officers, agents, representatives, and employees.

10. "Commerce" shall mean as defined in Section 4 of the Federal Trade Commission Act, 15 U.S.C. § 44.

I. IT IS ORDERED that respondent, directly or through any corporation, subsidiary, division, or other device, in connection with any online collection of personal information from children and/or consumers age thirteen (13) through seventeen (17), in or affecting commerce, shall not make any misrepresentation, in any manner, expressly or by implication:

A. That the information collected is maintained in an anonymous manner;

B. That children and/or consumers age thirteen (13) through seventeen (17) who submit such information will receive an e-mail newsletter or any other represented product or service;

C. That children and/or consumers age thirteen (13) through seventeen (17) who submit such information are eligible to win prizes in respondent's drawing or contest; or

D. Regarding the collection or use of personal information from or about children and/or consumers age thirteen (13) through seventeen (17).

II. IT IS FURTHER ORDERED that respondent, directly or through any corporation, subsidiary, division, or other device, in connection with the online collection of personal information at a website directed to children, or at any commercial website where respondent has actual knowledge that it is collecting personal information from a child, in or affecting commerce, shall not collect personal information from any child if respondent has actual knowledge that such child does not have his or her parent's permission to provide the information to respondent. For purposes of Parts II, III, IV, and V of this order, respondent shall not be deemed to have actual knowledge if the child has falsely represented that (s)he is not a child and respondent does not knowingly possess information that such representation is false.

III. IT IS FURTHER ORDERED that respondent, directly or through any corporation, subsidiary, division, or other device, in connection with the online collection of personal information from children, at a website directed to children, or at any commercial website where respondent has actual knowledge that it is collecting personal information from a child, in or affecting commerce, shall provide clear and prominent notice with respect to respondent's practices regarding its collection and use of personal information. Such notice shall include:

A. what information is being collected (*e.g.*, "name," "home address," "e-mail address," "age," "interests");

B. how respondent uses such information;

C. respondent's disclosure practices for such information (*e.g.*, parties to whom it may be disclosed, such as "advertisers of consumer products," "mailing list companies," "the general public");

D. a description of a means that is reasonable under the circumstances by which a parent whose child has provided personal information may obtain, upon request and upon proper identification, (i) a description of the specific types of personal information collected from the child by respondent, (ii) the opportunity at any time to refuse to permit the respondent's further use or maintenance in retrievable form, or future online collection, of personal information from that child, and (iii) any personal information collected from the child.

Such notice shall appear on the home page of respondent's website(s) directed to children, or at any commercial website where respondent has actual knowledge that it is collecting personal information from a child, and at each location on the site(s) at which such information is collected.

Provided, however, that for purposes of this Part, compliance with all of the following shall be deemed adequate notice: (a) placement of a clear and prominent hyperlink or button labeled "PRIVACY NOTICE" on the home page(s), which directly links to the privacy notice screen(s); (b) placement of the information required in this Part clearly and prominently on the privacy notice screen(s), followed on the same screen(s) with a button that must be clicked on to make it disappear; and (c) at each location on the site at which any personal information is collected, placement of a clear and prominent hyperlink on the initial screen on which the collection takes place, which links directly to the privacy notice and which is accompanied by the following statement in bold typeface:

NOTICE: WE COLLECT PERSONAL INFORMATION ON THIS SITE. TO LEARN MORE ABOUT HOW WE USE YOUR INFORMATION CLICK HERE.

IV. IT IS FURTHER ORDERED that respondent, directly or through any corporation, subsidiary, division, or other device, in connection with the online collection of personal information from children at a website directed to children, or at any commercial website where respondent has actual knowledge that it is collecting personal information from a child, in or affecting commerce, shall maintain a procedure by which it obtains verifiable parental consent for the collection, use or disclosure of such information from children.

V. IT IS FURTHER ORDERED that respondent Liberty Financial Companies, Inc., and its successors and assigns, shall delete from its website(s) directed to children, and at any commercial website(s) where respondent has actual knowledge that it is collecting personal information from a child, all personal information collected from children prior to the date of service of the order.

VI. IT IS FURTHER ORDERED that after the effective date of the Children's Online Privacy Protection Act of 1998 and any regulations or guides promulgated by the Commission pursuant to the Act, compliance with such statute, regulations, and guides shall be deemed to be compliance with the definition section of this order and Parts II, III and IV of this order.

VII. IT IS FURTHER ORDERED that respondent Liberty Financial Companies, Inc., and its successors and assigns, shall maintain and upon request make available to the Federal Trade Commission for inspection and copying the following:

A. For five (5) years after the last date of dissemination of a notice required by this order, a print or electronic copy in HTML format of all documents relating to compliance with Parts III through V of this order, including, but not limited to, a sample copy of every information collection form, Web page, screen, or document containing any representation regarding respondent's information collection and use practices pertaining to children. Each Web page copy shall be accompanied by the URL of the Web page where the material was posted online. Electronic copies shall include all text and graphics files, audio scripts, and other computer files used in presenting information on the World Wide Web; and

B. For five (5) years after the last collection of personal information from a child, all materials evidencing the verifiable parental consent given to respondent.

Provided, however, that after creation of any Web page or screen in compliance with this order, respondent shall not be required to retain a print or electronic copy of any amended Web page or screen to the extent that the amendment does not affect respondent's compliance obligations under this order.

VIII. IT IS FURTHER ORDERED that respondent Liberty Financial Companies, Inc., and its successors and assigns, shall deliver a copy of this order to all current and future principals, officers, directors, and managers, and to all current and future employees, agents, and representatives having responsibilities with respect to the subject matter of this order. Respondent shall deliver this order to current personnel within thirty (30) days after the date of service of this order, and to future personnel within thirty (30) days after the person assumes such position or responsibilities.

IX. IT IS FURTHER ORDERED that respondent Liberty Financial Companies, Inc., and its successors and assigns, shall notify the Commission at least thirty (30) days prior to any change in the corporation that may affect compliance obligations arising under this order, including, but not limited to, a dissolution, assignment, sale, merger, or other action that would result in the emergence of a successor corporation; the creation or dissolution of a subsidiary, parent, or affiliate that engages in any acts or practices subject to this order; the proposed filing of a bankruptcy petition; or a change in the corporate name or address.

Provided, however, that, with respect to any proposed change in the corporation about which respondent learns less than thirty (30) days prior to the date such action is to take place, respondent shall notify the Commission as soon as is practicable after obtaining such knowledge. All notices required by this Part shall be sent by certified mail to the Associate Director, Division of Enforcement, Bureau of Consumer Protection, Federal Trade Commission, Washington, D.C. 20580.

X. IT IS FURTHER ORDERED that respondent Liberty Financial Companies, Inc., and its successors and assigns, shall, within sixty (60) days after service of this order, and at such other times as the Federal Trade Commission may require, file with the Commission a report, in writing, setting forth in detail the manner and form in which they have complied with this order.

XI. This order will terminate twenty (20) years from the date of its issuance, or twenty (20) years from the most recent date that the United States or the Federal Trade Commission files a complaint (with or without an accompanying consent decree) in federal court alleging any violation of the order, whichever comes later; provided, however, that the filing of such a complaint will not affect the duration of:

A. Any Part in this order that terminates in less than twenty (20) years;

B. This order's application to any respondent that is not named as a defendant in such complaint; and

C. This order if such complaint is filed after the order has terminated pursuant to this Part.

Provided, further, that if such complaint is dismissed or a federal court rules that the respondent did not violate any provision of the order, and the dismissal or ruling is either not appealed or upheld on appeal, then the order will terminate according to this Part as though the complaint had never been filed, except that the order will not terminate between the date such complaint is filed and the later of the deadline for appealing such dismissal or ruling and the date such dismissal or ruling is upheld on appeal.

Signed this _____ day of _____, 1999.

[Signatures of Parties]

APPENDIX 10:
ELI LILLY AND COMPANY COMPLAINT

UNITED STATES OF AMERICA

FEDERAL TRADE COMMISSION

In the Matter of

ELI LILLY and COMPANY, a corporation.

DOCKET NO. C-4047

COMPLAINT

The Federal Trade Commission, having reason to believe that Eli Lilly and Company, a corporation ("respondent") has violated the provisions of the Federal Trade Commission Act, and it appearing to the Commission that this proceeding is in the public interest, alleges:

1. Respondent Eli Lilly and Company is an Indiana corporation with its principal office or place of business at Lilly Corporate Center, Indianapolis, Indiana 46285. Respondent, a pharmaceutical company, has advertised and promoted its anti-depressant medication, Prozac, through the company's Web sites www.prozac.com and www.lilly.com.

2. The acts and practices of respondent as alleged in this complaint have been in or affecting commerce, as "commerce" is defined in Section 4 of the Federal Trade Commission Act.

3. Respondent promotes its Prozac.com Web site as "Your Guide to Evaluating and Recovering from Depression." From March 15, 2000 until June 22, 2001, respondent advertised, promoted, and marketed via www.Prozac.com and www.Lilly.com an email reminder service known as "Medi-messenger." Consumers who utilized the Medi-messenger service could design and receive personal email reminder messages from respondent concerning their medication or other matters. Once a visitor registered for Medi-messenger, the re-

minder messages were automatically emailed from Prozac.com to the subscriber at the email address s/he provided, and according to the schedule established by the subscriber.

4. Subscribers to the Medi-messenger service registered by providing an email address, a password, the text of the reminder message they wanted to receive, and the schedule for sending the reminder messages. (Complaint Exhibit A, pp.1-4). After providing information to register for Medi-messenger, the subscriber was invited to view the Prozac.com "Privacy Statement" via a hyperlink, which was positioned just above the "Submit" and "Reset" buttons. (Complaint Exhibit A, p.4)

5. Respondent has disseminated or has caused to be disseminated privacy policies on Prozac.com and Lilly.com, including but not necessarily limited to the attached Exhibits B and C. These privacy policies contain the following statements regarding the privacy and confidentiality of personal information collected through respondent's Web sites:

A. Your Privacy

This Web site has been created to provide our visitors with information on certain medical conditions. Eli Lilly and Company respects the privacy of visitors to its Web sites, and we feel it is important to maintain our guests' privacy as they take advantage of this resource. As a result, we have developed this privacy code.

We will use Your Information to respond to requests you may make of us, and from time to time, we may refer to Your Information to better understand your needs and how we can improve our Web sites, products and services. Any and all uses would comply with all applicable laws. We may also use Your Information to contact you. However, the provision of Your Information will only be necessary if you choose to use or receive certain tools or services, such as a newsletter or our medical reminder service.

Our Web sites have security measures in place, including the use of industry standard secure socket layer encryption (SSL), to protect the confidentiality of any of Your Information that you volunteer; however, to take advantage of this your browser must support encryption protection (found in Internet Explorer release 3.0 and above). These security measures also help us to honor your choices for the use of Your Information.

B. Privacy

Eli Lilly and Company respects the privacy of visitors to its websites, and we feel it is important to maintain our guests' privacy as they take advantage of this resource. As a result, we have developed this privacy code.

We will use Your Information to respond to requests you may make of us, and from time to time, we may refer to Your Information to better understand your needs and how we can improve our Web sites, products and services. Any and all uses would comply with all applicable laws. We may also use Your Information to contact you in connection with your requests.

Our Web sites have security measures in place, including the use of industry standard secure socket layer encryption (SSL), to protect the confidentiality of any of Your Information that you volunteer; however, to take advantage of this your browser must support encryption protection (found in Internet Explorer release 3.0 and above).

6. On June 27, 2001, at respondent's direction, an Eli Lilly employee sent an email message to Medi-messenger subscribers announcing the termination of the Medi-messenger service. To do this, the employee created a new computer program to access subscribers' email addresses and send them the email. The June 27th email disclosed the email addresses of all 669 Medi-messenger subscribers to each individual subscriber by including all of the recipients' email addresses within the "To:" line of the message. (Complaint Exhibit D, email addresses redacted from original). By including the email addresses of all Medi-messenger subscribers within the June 27th email message, respondent unintentionally disclosed personal information provided to it by consumers in connection with their use of the Prozac.com Web site.

7. The June 27th disclosure of personal information resulted from respondent's failure to maintain or implement internal measures appropriate under the circumstances to protect sensitive consumer information. For example, respondent failed to provide appropriate training for its employees regarding consumer privacy and information security; failed to provide appropriate oversight and assistance for the employee who sent out the email, who had no prior experience in creating, testing, or implementing the computer program used; and failed to implement appropriate checks and controls on the process, such as reviewing the computer program with experienced personnel and pretesting the program internally before sending out the email. Respondent's failure to implement appropriate measures also violated certain of its own written policies.

8. Through the means described in Paragraph 5, respondent has represented, expressly or by implication, that it employs measures and takes steps appropriate under the circumstances to maintain and protect the privacy and confidentiality of personal information obtained from or about consumers through its Prozac.com and Lilly.com Web sites.

9. In truth and in fact, as described in Paragraphs 6 and 7, respondent has not employed measures and has not taken steps appropriate under

the circumstances to maintain and protect the privacy and confidentiality of personal information obtained from or about consumers through its Prozac.com and Lilly.com Web sites. Therefore, the representation set forth in Paragraph 8 was, and is, false or misleading.

10. The acts and practices of respondent as alleged in this complaint constitute unfair or deceptive acts or practices in or affecting commerce in violation of Section 5(a) of the Federal Trade Commission Act.

THEREFORE, the Federal Trade Commission this eighth day of May, 2002, has issued this complaint against respondent.

By the Commission.

Donald S. Clark

Secretary

APPENDIX 11:
ELI LILLY AND COMPANY CONSENT ORDER

UNITED STATES OF AMERICA
FEDERAL TRADE COMMISSION

In the Matter of	)	**FILE NO. 012 3214**
	)	
ELI LILLY AND COMPANY,	)	**AGREEMENT CONTAINING**
a corporation.	)	**CONSENT ORDER**
	)	

The Federal Trade Commission has conducted an investigation of certain acts and practices of Eli Lilly and Company, a corporation ("proposed respondent"). Proposed respondent, having been represented by counsel, is willing to enter into an agreement containing a consent order resolving the allegations contained in the attached draft complaint. Therefore,

IT IS HEREBY AGREED by and between Eli Lilly and Company, by its duly authorized officer, and counsel for the Federal Trade Commission that:

1.   Proposed respondent Eli Lilly and Company is an Indiana corporation with its principal office or place of business at Lilly Corporate Center, Indianapolis, Indiana 46285.

2.   Proposed respondent admits all the jurisdictional facts set forth in the draft complaint.

3.   Proposed respondent waives:

   (a)   Any further procedural steps;

   (b)   The requirement that the Commission's decision contain a statement of findings of fact and conclusions of law; and

   (c)   All rights to seek judicial review or otherwise to challenge or contest the validity of the order entered pursuant to this agreement.

4.   This agreement shall not become part of the public record of the proceeding unless and until it is accepted by the Commission. If this agreement is accepted by the Commission, it, together

Page 1 of 8

with the draft complaint, will be placed on the public record for a period of thirty (30) days and information about it publicly released. The Commission thereafter may either withdraw its acceptance of this agreement and so notify proposed respondent, in which event it will take such action as it may consider appropriate, or issue and serve its complaint (in such form as the circumstances may require) and decision in disposition of the proceeding.

5.   This agreement is for settlement purposes only and does not constitute an admission by proposed respondent that the law has been violated as alleged in the draft complaint, or that the facts as alleged in the draft complaint, other than the jurisdictional facts, are true.

6.   This agreement contemplates that, if it is accepted by the Commission, and if such acceptance is not subsequently withdrawn by the Commission pursuant to the provisions of Section 2.34 of the Commission's Rules, the Commission may, without further notice to proposed respondent, (1) issue its complaint corresponding in form and substance with the attached draft complaint and its decision containing the following order in disposition of the proceeding, and (2) make information about it public. When so entered, the order shall have the same force and effect and may be altered, modified, or set aside in the same manner and within the same time provided by statute for other orders. The order shall become final upon service. Delivery of the complaint and the decision and order to proposed respondent's address as stated in this agreement by any means specified in Section 4.4(a) of the Commission's Rules shall constitute service. Proposed respondent waives any right it may have to any other manner of service. The complaint may be used in construing the terms of the order. No agreement, understanding, representation, or interpretation not contained in the order or the agreement may be used to vary or contradict the terms of the order.

7.   Proposed respondent has read the draft complaint and consent order. It understands that it may be liable for civil penalties in the amount provided by law and other appropriate relief for each violation of the order after it becomes final.

<u>ORDER</u>

DEFINITIONS

For purposes of this order, the following definitions shall apply:

1.   "Personally identifiable information" or "personal information" shall mean individually identifiable information from or about an individual consumer including, but not limited to: (a) a first and last name; (b) a home or other physical address, including street name and name of city or town; (c) an email address or other online contact information, such as an instant messaging user identifier or a screen name that reveals an individual's email address; (d) a telephone number; (e) a social security number; (f) an Internet Protocol ("IP") address or host name that identifies an individual consumer; (g) a persistent identifier, such as a customer number held in a "cookie" or processor serial number, that is combined with other available data that identifies an individual consumer; or (h) or any information that is combined with (a) through (g) above. <u>Provided that</u>, this definition shall not include personally identifiable information about physicians, nurses, or other health care professionals, or their staff, that is collected in connection with such persons' professional duties.

2.   Unless otherwise specified, "respondent" shall mean Eli Lilly and Company, its successors and assigns and its officers, agents, representatives, and employees acting within the scope of their authority on behalf of, or in active concert or participation with, Eli Lilly and Company.

3.   "Lilly USA division" shall mean Lilly USA, a division of Eli Lilly and Company, and Lilly USA's successors, assigns, officers, representatives, agents, employees, and other entities responsible for the development, control, support, or oversight of U.S. product or service sales, advertising, or marketing, information management, or information technology. <u>Provided that</u>, the Lilly USA division shall be treated as a corporation under the control of Eli Lilly and Company for the purpose of determining whether any other entity is Lilly USA division's successor or assign.

4.   "Commerce" shall mean as defined in Section 4 of the Federal Trade Commission Act, 15 U.S.C. § 44.

I.

IT IS ORDERED that respondent shall not misrepresent in any manner, expressly or by implication, the extent to which it maintains and protects the privacy or confidentiality of any personally identifiable information collected from or about consumers, in connection with the advertising, marketing, offering for sale or sale, in or affecting commerce, of any pharmaceutical, medical or other

Page 3 of 8

health-related product or service by respondent's Lilly USA division, directly or through any corporation, subsidiary, division, or other entity.

II.

IT IS FURTHER ORDERED that respondent shall establish and maintain an information security program for the protection of personally identifiable information collected from or about consumers in connection with the advertising, marketing, offering for sale, or sale of any pharmaceutical, medical, or other health-related product or service, in or affecting commerce, by respondent's Lilly USA division, directly or through any corporation, subsidiary, division, or other entity. Such program shall consist of:

A. designating appropriate personnel to coordinate and oversee the program;

B. identifying reasonably foreseeable internal and external risks to the security, confidentiality, and integrity of personal information, including any such risks posed by lack of training, and addressing these risks in each relevant area of its operations, whether performed by employees or agents, including: (i) management and training of personnel; (ii) information systems for the processing, storage, transmission, or disposal of personal information; and (iii) prevention and response to attacks, intrusions, unauthorized access, or other information systems failures;

C. conducting an annual written review by qualified persons, within ninety (90) days after the date of service of this order and yearly thereafter. which review shall monitor and document compliance with the program, evaluate the program's effectiveness, and recommend changes to it; and

D. adjusting the program in light of any findings and recommendations resulting from reviews or ongoing monitoring, and in light of any material changes to its operations that affect the program.

III.

IT IS FURTHER ORDERED that respondent shall for a period of five (5) years after the date of service of this order maintain and upon request make available to the Federal Trade Commission for inspection and copying a print or electronic copy of the following documents relating to

Page 4 of 8

compliance with Parts I and II of this order by respondent's Lilly USA division, directly or through any corporation, subsidiary, division, or other entity:

A.   a sample copy of each different consumer-targeted print, broadcast, cable, or Internet advertisement, promotion, information collection form, Web page, screen, email message, or other document containing any representation regarding the Lilly USA division's collection, use, and security of personal information from or about consumers. Each Web page copy shall be dated and contain the full URL of the Web page where the material was posted online. Electronic copies shall include all text and graphics files, audio scripts, and other computer files used in presenting the information on the Web. Provided, however, that after creation of any Web page or screen in compliance with this order, the Lilly USA division shall not be required to retain a print or electronic copy of any amended Web page or screen to the extent that the amendment does not affect its compliance obligations under this order;

B.   all reports, studies, reviews, audits, audit trails, policies, training materials, and plans, whether prepared by or on behalf of respondent, relating to the Lilly USA division's compliance with the information security program required by Part II of this order; and

C.   any documents, whether prepared by or on behalf of the Lilly USA division, that contradict, qualify, or call into question its compliance with the information security program required by Part II of this order, maintained through reasonable efforts in accordance with a document retention program.

IV.

IT IS FURTHER ORDERED that respondent Eli Lilly and Company, and its successors and assigns, shall deliver a copy of this order to all current and future principals, officers, directors, and managers, and to all current and future employees, agents, and representatives having responsibilities relating to the subject matter of this order. Respondent shall deliver this order to such current personnel within thirty (30) days after the date of service of this order, and to such future personnel within thirty (30) days after the person assumes such position or responsibilities.

Page 5 of 8

V.

IT IS FURTHER ORDERED that respondent Eli Lilly and Company, and its successors and assigns, shall notify the Commission at least thirty (30) days prior to any change in the corporation that may affect compliance obligations arising under this order, including, but not limited to, a dissolution, assignment, sale, merger, or other action that would result in the emergence of a successor corporation; the creation or dissolution of a subsidiary, parent, or affiliate that engages in any acts or practices subject to this order; the proposed filing of a bankruptcy petition; or a change in the corporate name or address. Provided, however, that, with respect to any proposed change in the corporation about which respondent learns less than thirty (30) days prior to the date such action is to take place, respondent shall notify the Commission as soon as is practicable after obtaining such knowledge. All notices required by this Part shall be sent by certified mail to the Associate Director, Division of Enforcement, Bureau of Consumer Protection, Federal Trade Commission, Washington, D.C. 20580.

VI.

IT IS FURTHER ORDERED that respondent Eli Lilly and Company, and its successors and assigns, shall within one hundred and twenty (120) days after service of this order, and at such other times as the Federal Trade Commission may require, file with the Commission a report, in writing, setting forth in detail the manner and form in which they have complied with this order. This report shall include a copy of the initial annual review required by Part II.C of this order.

VII.

This order will terminate twenty (20) years from the date of its issuance, or twenty (20) years from the most recent date that the United States or the Federal Trade Commission files a complaint (with or without an accompanying consent decree) in federal court alleging any violation of the order, whichever comes later; provided, however, that the filing of such a complaint will not affect the duration of:

A. Any Part in this order that terminates in less than twenty (20) years;

B. This order's application to any respondent that is not named as a defendant in such complaint; and

C. This order if such complaint is filed after the order has terminated pursuant to this Part.

Page 6 of 8

<u>Provided, further,</u> that if such complaint is dismissed or a federal court rules that the respondent did not violate any provision of the order, and the dismissal or ruling is either not appealed or upheld on appeal, then the order will terminate according to this Part as though the complaint had never been filed, except that the order will not terminate between the date such complaint is filed and the later of the deadline for appealing such dismissal or ruling and the date such dismissal or ruling is upheld on appeal.

Signed this _____ day of _____, 2002.

ELI LILLY AND COMPANY

By: _____

REBECCA O. KENDALL
Senior Vice President and General Counsel
Eli Lilly and Company

_____

KAREN E. SILVERMAN
Latham & Watkins
Counsel for Respondent Eli Lilly and Company

FEDERAL TRADE COMMISSION

_____

MAMIE KRESSES
Counsel for the Federal Trade Commission

_____

Page 7 of 8

DEAN C. FORBES
Counsel for the Federal Trade Commission

Page 8 of 8

APPROVED:

MARY KOELBEL ENGLE
Acting Associate Director
Division of Advertising Practices

J. HOWARD BEALES, III
Director
Bureau of Consumer Protection

APPENDIX 12:
TOYSMART.COM COMPLAINT

UNITED STATES DISTRICT COURT

DISTRICT OF MASSACHUSETTS

FEDERAL TRADE COMMISSION,
600 Pennsylvania Ave., N.W.,
Washington, DC 20580, Plaintiff,

v.

TOYSMART.COM, LLC,
170 High Street
Waltham, MA, 02453
a Delaware corporation, Defendants.

CIVIL ACTION NO. 00-11341-RGS

FIRST AMENDED COMPLAINT FOR PERMANENT INJUNCTION AND OTHER EQUITABLE RELIEF

Plaintiff, the Federal Trade Commission ("FTC" or "Commission"), by its undersigned attorneys, alleges:

JURISDICTION AND VENUE

1. This Court has subject matter jurisdiction over the FTC's claims pursuant to 15 U.S.C. §§ 45(a) and 53(b) and 28 U.S.C. §§ 1331, 1337(a) and 1345.

2. Venue in this District is proper under 15 U.S.C. § 53(b) and 28 U.S.C. § 1391(b) and (c).

THE PARTIES

3. Plaintiff, the FTC, is an independent agency of the United States government created by statute. 15 U.S.C. §§ 41 et seq. The Commission enforces

Section 5(a) of the FTC Act, 15 U.S.C. § 45(a), which prohibits unfair or deceptive acts or practices in or affecting commerce. The Commission may initiate federal district court proceedings to enjoin violations of the FTC Act and to secure such equitable relief as is appropriate in each case. 15 U.S.C. § 53(b). The Commission also enforces the Children's Online Privacy Protection Act of 1998 (COPPA), 15 U.S.C. § 6501 et seq.

4. Defendants Toysmart.com, Inc. and Toysmart.com, LLC (collectively "Toysmart" or "defendant") are Delaware corporations. Toysmart.com, Inc. was incorporated on November 23, 1998, and qualified by the Secretary of State of Massachusetts on December 15, 1998; Toysmart.com, LLC was incorporated on August 8, 1999. Toysmart's principal place of business is located at 170 High Street, Waltham, MA 02453. Toysmart is the operator of a Web site on the Internet, located at www.toysmart.com, that is a retail toystore. Toysmart transacts or has transacted business in this district.

COMMERCE

5. At all times material to this complaint, defendant's course of business, including the acts and practices alleged herein, has been and is in or affecting commerce, as "commerce" is defined in Section 4 of the FTC Act, 15 U.S.C. § 44.

DEFENDANTS' BUSINESS PRACTICES

6. Since at least January 1999, Toysmart has advertised, promoted, and sold toys on the Internet, located at www.toysmart.com. Toysmart markets its products and services throughout the United States and the world via the Internet.

7. In connection with its Web site, Toysmart collects personal customer information including, but not limited to, consumers' names, addresses, billing information, shopping preferences, and family profile information ("Customer Lists").

8. In September 1999, Toysmart became a licensee of TRUSTe, an organization that certifies the privacy policies of online businesses and allows such businesses to display a TRUSTe trustmark or seal.

9. From September 1999 to the present, the privacy policy posted on the Toysmart.com Web site has stated, *inter alia*, (1) "Personal information voluntarily submitted by visitors to our site, such as name, address, billing information and shopping preferences, is never shared with a third party. All information obtained by toysmart.com is used only to personalize your experience online;" and (2) "When you register with toysmart.com, you can rest assured that your information will never be shared with a third

party." A true and correct copy of the Toysmart privacy policy is attached hereto as Exhibit 1.

10. On May 22, 2000, Toysmart announced that, as of midnight on May 19, 2000, it had officially ceased operations. Toysmart also announced that it had retained the services of a Boston-based management consultant, The Recovery Group, to locate parties interested in acquiring Toysmart.com's business and assets.

11. On May 22, 2000, Toysmart began soliciting bids for the purchase of its assets. Bids have been sought for the purchase of all of the company's assets or for individual assets. Among the individual assets offered for sale by Toysmart.com are its Customer Lists (on either an exclusive or non-exclusive basis). Other assets available include inventory; warehouse fixtures and equipment; intangible assets including domain name, product databases, and Web site source code; and a B2B business plan. Bids were due to Toysmart by 6:00 p.m. EST on June 19, 2000.

12. On June 9, 2000, Toysmart's creditors filed a petition for involuntary bankruptcy. *See* In Re: Toysmart.com, LLC, No. 00-13995-CJK (Bankr. D. Mass).

13. On June 19, 2000, bidding for Toysmart's assets concluded. Toysmart informed the Federal Trade Commission that its Customer Lists will not be transferred to a third party absent bankruptcy court approval.

14. Beginning May 1, 2000, Toysmart collected personal information from children on its Web site through a dinosaur trivia contest. This information included name, email address, and age.

15. The trivia contest was directed to children. The trivia contest included no mechanism for parental notification or consent prior to the collection of information from children under the age of 13.

VIOLATIONS OF SECTION 5 OF THE FTC ACT

COUNT I

16. Section 5(a) of the FTC Act, 15 U.S.C.§ 45(a), prohibits "unfair or deceptive acts or practices in or affecting commerce."

17. From at least September 1999 to the present, defendant Toysmart, directly or through its employees and agents, in connection with its collection of personal consumer information, expressly and/or by implication, represented that it would "never" disclose, sell, or offer for sale customers' or registered members' personal information to third parties.

18. In truth and in fact, Toysmart has disclosed, sold, or offered for sale its customer lists and profiles. Therefore, the representation set forth in Paragraph 17 was, and is, a deceptive practice.

VIOLATIONS OF THE CHILDREN'S ONLINE PRIVACY PROTECTION ACT

COUNT II

19. Since at least May 1, 2000, through its dinosaur trivia contest, which was directed to children, Toysmart collected personal information from children that, in addition, it actually knew to be under the age of 13, without providing notice to parents or obtaining verifiable parental consent prior to the collection of such personal information. The information collected included name, email address, and age.

20. The practice set forth in Paragraph 19 did not fall within the exception to prior parental consent of 16 C.F.R. § 312.5(c)(2) and therefore was, and is, a violation of the Children's Online Privacy Protection Act, 15 U.S.C. § 6503 and 16 C.F.R. §§ 312.3-312.5.

CONSUMER INJURY

21. Toysmart's conduct, as set forth in Paragraphs 6-21 will injure consumers throughout the United States by invading their privacy.

22. Absent injunctive relief by this Court, the defendant is likely to injure consumers and harm the public interest.

THIS COURT'S POWER TO GRANT RELIEF

23. This Court is empowered by Section 13(b) of the FTC Act, 15 U.S.C. § 53(b), to grant injunctive and other ancillary relief, to prevent and remedy any violations of any provision of law enforced by the Commission.

PRAYER FOR RELIEF

WHEREFORE plaintiff Federal Trade Commission pursuant to Section 13(b) of the FTC Act, 15 U.S.C.§ 53(b) and the Court's own equitable powers, requests that this Court:

1. Permanently and preliminarily enjoin defendant from violating the FTC Act, as alleged herein;

2. Declare Toysmart's transfer of the Customer Lists to any third party to be a violation of the FTC Act;

3. Permanently and preliminarily enjoin defendant from violating the COPPA;

4. Require Toysmart to delete or destroy information collected in violation of COPPA;

5. Award such other relief as the Court finds necessary to redress injury to consumers resulting from defendant's violations of the FTC Act and COPPA.

Respectfully submitted,

Attorneys

Federal Trade Commission
601 Pennsylvania Ave., NW
Washington, DC 20580

(202) 326-3424/(202) 326-3296

Dated:

APPENDIX 13:
TOYSMART.COM CONSENT ORDER

UNITED STATES DISTRICT COURT

DISTRICT OF MASSACHUSETTS

FEDERAL TRADE COMMISSION,
600 Pennsylvania Ave., N.W.,
Washington, DC 20580, Plaintiff,

v.

TOYSMART.COM, LLC,
170 High Street
Waltham, MA, 02453
a Delaware corporation, Defendants.

CIVIL ACTION NO. 00-11341-RGS

STIPULATED CONSENT AGREEMENT AND FINAL ORDER

On July 10, 2000, plaintiff, the Federal Trade Commission ("Commission" or "FTC") commenced this action by filing its complaint against defendants Toysmart.com, LLC and Toysmart.com, Inc. (collectively, "Toysmart" or "Defendants"). The Complaint alleges that Toysmart engaged in deceptive acts or practices in violation of Section 5 of the Federal Trade Commission Act ("FTC Act"), 15 U.S.C. § 45(a), by disclosing, selling or offering for sale personal customer information, contrary to the terms of its privacy policy that personal information would never be disclosed to third parties. The Complaint seeks a permanent injunction and other equitable relief pursuant to Section 13(b) of the FTC Act, 15 U.S.C. § 53(b).

The Commission and the Defendants, by and through their counsel, have agreed to settlement of this action upon the following terms and conditions, without adjudication of any issues of fact or law.

IT IS THEREFORE ORDERED, ADJUDGED, AND DECREED as follows:

FINDINGS

1. This Court has jurisdiction over the subject matter of this case and has jurisdiction over Defendants. Venue in this district is proper.

2. The Commission has the authority under Section 13(b) of the FTC Act, 15 U.S.C. § 53(b), to seek the relief it has requested.

3. The Complaint states a claim upon which injunctive relief may be granted against the Defendants under Sections 5(a) and 13(b) of the FTC Act, 15 U.S.C. §§ 45(a) and 53(b).

4. Defendants' activities are in or affecting commerce, as defined in 15 U.S.C. § 44.

5. Defendants waive all rights to seek judicial review or otherwise challenge or contest the validity of this Order. Defendants also waive any claim that they may have held under the Equal Access to Justice Act, 28 U.S.C. § 2412, amended by Pub. L. 104-121, 110 Stat. 847, 863-64 (1996), concerning prosecution of this action to the date of this Order.

6. This agreement is for settlement purposes only and does not constitute an admission by Defendants that the law has been violated as alleged in the Complaint or that the facts as alleged in the Complaint are true.

7. Entry of the Final Order is in the public interest.

DEFINITIONS

For purposes of this Order:

1. "Defendants" means Toysmart.com, LLC and Toysmart.com, Inc.

2. "Customer Information" means information of or relating to consumers collected by Toysmart, including, but not limited to, name, address, billing information, shopping preferences, order history, gift registry selections, family profile information, and information about consumers' children, such as name, gender, birthday, and toy interests.

3. "Third Party" shall mean any individual, firm, or organization other than a Qualified Buyer and its successors, except to the extent that disclosure of Customer Information to such an individual, firm, or organization is necessary to maintain the technical functioning of the Toysmart Web site or to fulfill a consumer's request. "Third Party" includes any affiliates of a Qualified Buyer.

4. "Qualified Buyer"shall mean an entity that (1) concentrates its business in the family commerce market, involving the areas of education, toys, learning, home and/or instruction, including commerce, content, product and services, and (2) expressly agrees to the obligations set forth in the Stipulation and Order Establishing Conditions on Sale of Customer Information, entered by the Honorable Carol J. Kenner, Bankruptcy Judge for the United States Bankruptcy Court for the District of Massachusetts, on July ___, 2000, in In re: Toysmart.com, LLC, Case. No. 00-13995-CJK (the "Bankruptcy Order"), attached hereto as Exhibit A.

I. PROHIBITION AGAINST MISREPRESENTATIONS

IT IS HEREBY ORDERED that Defendants and their officers, agents, servants, employees, and those persons in active concert or participation with them who receive actual notice of this Order by personal service or otherwise, whether acting directly or through any corporation, subsidiary, division, or other device, are hereby restrained and enjoined from violating Section 5(a) of the FTC Act, 15 U.S.C. § 45(a), by:

A. Making, or assisting in making, directly or by implication, in connection with the collection of Customer Information, any false or misleading representation about whether such information will be shared with Third Parties; and

B. Disclosing, selling or offering for sale to any Third Party, any Customer Information collected by Defendants, except as expressly provided in the Bankruptcy Order.

II. REQUIREMENT THAT DEFENDANTS DELETE PERSONAL CUSTOMER INFORMATION

IT IS FURTHER ORDERED that, absent approval by the Bankruptcy Court on or before July 31, 2001, of the sale of the Customer Information to a Qualified Buyer or of a reorganization plan, Defendants and their officers, agents, servants, and employees shall, on or before August 31, 2001, delete or destroy all Customer Information in their possession, custody or control, and provide written confirmation to the FTC, sworn to under penalty of perjury, that all such Customer Information has been deleted or destroyed.

III. REQUIREMENT THAT DEFENDANTS COMPLY WITH THE CHILDREN'S ONLINE PRIVACY PROTECTION ACT

IT IS HEREBY ORDERED that Defendants and their officers, agents, servants, employees, and those persons in active concert or participation with them who receive actual notice of this Order by personal service or otherwise, whether acting directly or through any corporation, subsidiary, division, or other device, are hereby restrained and enjoined from violating the Children's Online Privacy Protection Act of 1998, 15 U.S.C. §§ 6501 et seq. and its implementing regulations, and are hereby required to delete or destroy any and all information collected in violation of 16 C.F.R. Part 312 et seq. within ten (10) days of the entry of this Order.

IV. FTC'S RIGHT TO FILE ACTION

IT IS FURTHER ORDERED that the Commission's agreement to and the Court's approval of this Order is expressly premised upon the truthfulness, accuracy, and completeness of the declaration sworn to under penalty of perjury provided by Toysmart and attached hereto as Exhibit B, stating that after diligent investigation it is not aware of any disclosures of customer information to third parties or other material violations of the Toysmart Privacy Statement prior to May 22, 2000, as the Commission relied upon this material information in negotiating and agreeing to the terms of this Order.

IT IS FURTHER ORDERED that nothing shall preclude the Commission from filing an action against Toysmart in this Court within the next one (1) year from the date of this Order, should the Commission subsequently obtain evidence that Toysmart in the above-referenced declaration failed to disclose a material violation of the Toysmart Privacy Statement, or made any other material misrepresentation or omission.

V. DOCUMENT RETENTION

IT IS FURTHER ORDERED that Defendants shall maintain for at least one (1) year from the date of service of this Order and, upon written request by FTC employees, make available to the FTC for inspection and copying:

A. All records and documents necessary to demonstrate fully their compliance with each provision of this Order;

B. A sample copy of any advertising and promotional material, including e-mail, regarding the sale of Defendants' tangible and intangible assets, other than the sale of such assets in the bankruptcy case; and

C . Copies of any complaints received by Defendants regarding Defendants' alleged disclosure, sale or offering for sale of personal customer information.

VI. NOTICE TO RELATED PERSONS AND ENTITIES

IT IS FURTHER ORDERED that, for a period of one (1) year from the date of entry of this Order, Defendants shall:

A. Deliver a copy of this Order to all of Defendants' current and future principals, officers, directors, and managers, and to all of Defendants' current and future employees, agents, and representatives having responsibilities with respect to the subject matter of this Order, and shall secure from each such person a signed and dated statement acknowledging receipt of the Order. Defendants shall deliver this Order to their current personnel within thirty (30) days after the date of service of this Order, and to their future personnel within thirty (30) days after the person assumes such position or responsibilities; and

B. Maintain for a period of one (1) year after creation, and upon reasonable notice, make available to representatives of the Commission, the original signed and dated acknowledgments of the receipt of copies of the Order.

VII. COMPLIANCE REPORTING AND MONITORING

IT IS FURTHER ORDERED that, in order that compliance with the provisions of this Order may be monitored:

A. Sixty (60) days after the date of entry of this Order, Defendants shall provide a written report to the FTC, sworn to under penalty of perjury, setting forth in detail the manner and form in which they have complied and are complying with this Order;

B. For the purposes of this Order, Defendants shall, unless otherwise directed by the Commission's authorized representatives, mail all written notifications to the Commission to:

Associate Director, Division of Financial Practices
Federal Trade Commission
600 Pennsylvania Ave., N.W.
Washington, D.C. 20580

Re: *FTC v. Toysmart.com*

C. The Commission is authorized, without further leave of Court, for a period of one (1) year from the date of entry of this Order, to obtain discovery from any person in the manner provided by Chapter V of the Federal Rules of Civil Procedure, Fed. R. Civ. P. 26-37, including the use of compulsory process pursuant to Fed. R. Civ. P. 45, for the purpose of monitoring and investigating Defendants' compliance with any provision of this Order;

D. The Commission is authorized to use representatives posing as consumers and suppliers to Defendants, Defendants' employees, or any other entity managed or controlled in whole or in part by defendants, without the necessity of identification or prior notice;

E. Nothing in this Order shall limit the Commission's lawful use of compulsory process, pursuant to Sections 9 and 20 of the FTC Act, 15 U.S.C. §§ 49 and 57b-1, to investigate whether defendants have violated any provision of this Order or Section 5 of the FTC Act, 15 U.S.C. § 45;

F. For a period of one (1) year from the date of entry of this Order, for the purpose of further determining compliance with this Order, Defendants shall permit representatives of the Commission, within three (3) business days of receipt of written notice from the Commission, access during normal business hours to any office or facility within the Defendants' custody, possession, or control storing documents and to permit inspection and copying of all documents within the Defendants' custody, possession or control relevant to any matter contained in this Order.

VIII. RETENTION OF JURISDICTION

IT IS FURTHER ORDERED that the Court retains jurisdiction of this matter for all purposes, including the construction, modification, and enforcement of this Order.

Signed this _____ day of _____, 2000.

[Signatures of Parties]

APPENDIX 14:
DIRECTORY OF STATE CONSUMER
PROTECTION AGENCIES

STATE	ADDRESS	TELEPHONE NUMBER
Alabama	Consumer Protection Division Office of the Attorney General 11 S. Union Street Montgomery, AL 36130	205-261-7334
Alaska	Consumer Protection Section Office of the Attorney General 1031 W. 4th Avenue, Suite 110-B Anchorage, AK 99501	907-279-0428
Arizona	Financial Fraud Division Office of the Attorney General 1275 W. Washington St. Phoenix, AZ 85007	602-542-3702
Arkansas	Consumer Protection Division Office of the Attorney General 200 Tower Building, 4th & Center Streets Little Rock, AR 72201	501-682-2007
California	Public Inquiry Unit Office of the Attorney General 1515 K Street, Suite 511 Sacramento, CA 94244-2550	916-322-3360
California	Consumer Protection Division Los Angeles City Attorney's Office 200 N. Main Street 1600 City Hall East Los Angeles, CA 90012	213-485-4515

STATE	ADDRESS	TELEPHONE NUMBER
Colorado	Consumer Protection Unit Office of the Attorney General 1525 Sherman Street, 3rd Floor Denver, CO 80203	303-866-5167
Connecticut	Department of Consumer Protection 165 Capitol Avenue Hartford, CT 06106	203-566-4999
Delaware	Division of Consumer Affairs Department of Community Affairs 820 N. French Street, 4th Floor, Wilmington, DE 19801	302-571-3250
District of Columbia	Department of Consumer & Regulatory Affairs 614 H Street NW Washington, DC 20001	202-737-7000
Florida	Division of Consumer Services 218 Mayo Building Tallahassee, FL 32399	904-488-2226
Georgia	Governor's Office of Consumer Affairs 2 Martin Luther King Jr. Drive SE Plaza Level, E Tower Atlanta, GA 30334	404-656-7000
Hawaii	Office of Consumer Protection 828 Fort St. Mall Honolulu, HI 96812-3767	808-548-2560
Idaho	None Listed	
Illinois	Consumer Protection Division Office of the Attorney General 100 W. Randolph Street, 12th Floor Chicago, IL 60601	312-917-3580
Indiana	Consumer Protection Division Office of the Attorney General 219 State House Indianapolis, IN 46204	317-232-6330
Iowa	Consumer Protection Division Office of the Attorney General 1300 E. Walnut Street, 2nd Floor, Des Moines, IA 50319	515-281-5926

STATE	ADDRESS	TELEPHONE NUMBER
Kansas	Consumer Protection Division Office of the Attorney General Kansas Judicial Center, 2nd Floor Topeka, KS 66612	913-296-3761
Kentucky	Consumer Protection Division Office of the Attorney General 209 St. Clair Street Frankfort, KY 40601	502-564-2200
Louisiana	Consumer Protection Section Office of the Attorney General State Capitol Building P.O. Box 94005 Baton Rouge, LA 70804	504-342-7013
Maine	Consumer and Antitrust Division Office of the Attorney General State House Station #6 Augusta, ME 04333	207-289-3716
Maryland	Consumer Protection Division Office of the Attorney General 7 N. Calvert Street, 3rd Floor, Baltimore, MD 21202	301-528-8662
Massachusetts	Consumer Protection Division Office of the Attorney General One Ashburton Place, Room 1411 Boston, MA 02108	617-727-7780
Michigan	Consumer Protection Division Office of the Attorney General 670 Law Building Lansing, MI 48913	517-373-1140
Minnesota	Office of Consumer Services Office of the Attorney General 117 University Avenue St. Paul, MN 55155	612-296-2331
Mississippi	Consumer Protection Division Office of the Attorney General P.O. Box 220 Jackson, MS 39205	601-359-3680
Missouri	Trade Offense Division Office of the Attorney General P.O. Box 899 Jefferson City, MO 65102	314-751-2616

STATE	ADDRESS	TELEPHONE NUMBER
Montana	Consumer Affairs Unit Department of Commerce 1424 9th Avenue Helena, MT 59620	406-444-4312
Nebraska	Consumer Protection Division Department of Justice 2115 State Capitol P.O. Box 98920 Lincoln, NE 68509	402-471-4723
Nevada	Department of Commerce State Mail Room Complex Las Vegas, NV 89158	702-486-4150
New Hampshire	Consumer Protection and Antitrust Division Office of the Attorney General State House Annex Concord, NH 03301	603-271-3641
New Jersey	Division of Consumer Affairs 1100 Raymond Boulevard, Room 504, Newark, NJ 07102	201-648-4010
New Mexico	Consumer and Economic Crime Division Office of the Attorney General P.O. Box Drawer 1508 Santa Fe, NM 87504	505-872-6910
New York	Consumer Protection Board 99 Washington Avenue Albany, NY 12210	518-474-8583
New York	Consumer Protection Board 250 Broadway, 17th Floor New York, NY 10007-2593	212-587-4908
North Carolina	Consumer Protection Section Office of the Attorney General P.O. Box 629 Raleigh, NC 27602	919-733-7741
North Dakota	Consumer Fraud Division Office of the Attorney General State Capitol Building Bismarck, ND 58505	701-224-2210

STATE	ADDRESS	TELEPHONE NUMBER
Ohio	Consumer Frauds and Crimes Section Office of the Attorney General 30 E. Broad Street, 25th Floor Columbus, OH 43266-0410	614-466-4986
Oklahoma	Consumer Affairs Office of the Attorney General 112 State Capitol Building Oklahoma City, OK 73105	405-521-3921
Oregon	Financial Fraud Section Office of the Attorney General Justice Building Salem, OR 97310	503-378-4320
Pennsylvania	Bureau of Consumer Protection Office of the Attorney General Strawberry Square, 14th Floor Harrisburg, PA 17120	717-787-9707
Rhode Island	Consumer Protection Division Office of the Attorney General 72 Pine Street Providence, RI 02903	401-277-2104
South Carolina	Department of Consumer Affairs P.O. Box 5757 Columbia, SC 29250	803-734-9452
South Dakota	Division of Consumer Affairs Office of the Attorney General State Capitol Building Pierre, SD 57501	605-773-4400
Tennessee	Division of Consumer Affairs Department of Commerce & Insurance 500 James Robertson Parkway, 5th Floor Nashville, Tn 37219	615-741-4737
Texas	Consumer Protection Division Office of the Attorney General Box 12548, Capitol Station Austin, TX 78711	512-463-2070
Utah	Division of Consumer Protection Department of Business Regulation 160 E. Third South P.O. Box 45802 Salt Lake City, UT 84145	801-530-6601

STATE	ADDRESS	TELEPHONE NUMBER
Vermont	Public Protection Division Office of the Attorney General 109 State Street Montpelier, VT 05602	802-828-3171
Virginia	Division of Consumer Counsel Office of the Attorney General Supreme Court Building 101 N. 8th Street Richmond, VA 23219	804-786-2116
Washington	Consumer and Business Fair Practices Division 710 2nd Avenue, Suite 1300 Seattle, WA 98104	206-464-7744
West Virginia	Consumer Protection Division Office of the Attorney General 812 Quarrier Street, 6th Floor Charleston, WV 25301	304-348-8986
Wisconsin	Office of Consumer Protection Department of Justice P.O. Box 7856 Madison, WI 53707	608-266-1852
Wyoming	Office of the Attorney General 123 State Capitol Building Cheyenne, WY 82002	307-777-6286

Source: Consumers Resource Handbook, U.S. Office of Consumer Affairs

APPENDIX 15:
INSTRUCTIONS FOR SETTING COOKIES PREFERENCES

NETSCAPE NAVIGATOR 4.X

1. Go to the Edit menu and select Preferences.

2. Click on the Advanced heading.

3. Go to Cookies and click on the option you want:

   (a) Accept all cookies;

   (b) Accept only cookies that get sent back to the originating server; or

   (c) Disable cookies.

4. You may also check "Warn me before accepting a cookie" if you want your browser to ask your permission before downloading a cookie.

INTERNET EXPLORER 5

1. Go to the Tools menu and select Internet Options.

2. Click on the Security tab.

3. Click on the Custom Level button.

4. Scroll down to the Cookies heading.

5. Click on the options you want for stored and non-stored cookies.

6. Click on Disable to reject all cookies.

7. Click on Enable to accept all cookies.

8. Click on Prompt to ensure that you'll be asked permission before accepting a cookie.

INTERNET EXPLORER 4 AND 5 ON MACINTOSH

1. Go to the Edit menu and select Preferences.

2. Click on the Receiving Files tab.

3. Click on the Cookies heading.

4. Scroll down to the Cookies heading.

5. On the right side of the window, there is a pull-down menu, preceded by "When receiving cookies" followed by the following options:

(a) Never Ask: Cookies are always accepted and you are never prompted before a cookie is saved to your hard disk.

(b) Ask For Each Site: For each site you are asked whether you want to accept or decline cookies from the site.

(c) Ask For Each Cookie: As each cookie arrives, you are asked if you want to accept it.

(d) Never Accept: Cookies are never accepted and you are never prompted.

6. Select the most appropriate option from above.

7. Click OK

MAKING YOUR COOKIES FOLDER READ ONLY

This method allows you to accept cookies, but it limits the amount of information Web sites can obtain and prevents sites from writing documents onto your hard disk.

1. Double click the My Computer icon on your desktop.

2. Locate the Cookies folder on your computer's hard disk. The folder is usually found in the C:\WINDOWS directory.

3. Open the folder by double clicking on it.

4. Delete all the files without the .txt suffix (these are the cookies) in the folder. The files with the .txt suffix are system files.

5. Close the Cookies folder.

6. In the C:\WINDOWS directory, click once on the Cookies folder.

7. Select Properties from the File menu.

8. Mark the Read Only box under the Attributes heading and click OK.

Source: Better Business Bureau Online.

APPENDIX 16:
AMERICAN EXPRESS INTERNET PRIVACY STATEMENT

INTERNET PRIVACY STATEMENT

About the Company

American Express is a diversified worldwide travel, financial and network services provider founded in 1850. The company is a leader in charge and credit cards, stored value products, travel services, financial planning, investment products, insurance and international banking. In each of these businesses, we have relationships with customers—individuals to whom we provide personal financial products and services.

As a part of these customer relationships, we collect information necessary to enroll customers in products and services, to provide the services they have selected, to administer their accounts, and to offer them related or additional American Express products and services.

American Express respects your privacy and is committed to protecting it at all times. This Internet Privacy Statement explains how we collect, use, and safeguard information on this Web site.

TRACKING ACTIVITY ON OUR WEBSITE

When you browse americanexpress.com and have not registered for any online service from American Express, you browse anonymously. Personally identifiable information—such as your name, address, phone number, and e-mail address—is not collected as you browse.

However, we track how our site is used by both anonymous visitors and our registered customers. One way we track is by using a small string of text that is sent to your browser known as a "cookie." Cookies collect information that includes the server your computer is logged onto, your browser type (for example, Netscape or Internet Explorer), and whether you responded to an American Express banner ad from outside our site or through an e-mail link. A cookie cannot retrieve any other data from your hard drive, pass on computer viruses, or capture your e-mail address or any other personally identifiable information. Please note that accepting cookies is required if you want to view personal or confidential information online, because they are essential for site administration and security.

Another way we track site activity is by using transparent electronic images called "clear GIFs," "Web bugs," or "Web beacons" on americanexpress.com Web pages. These images count the number of users who visit that page from specific banner ads outside americanexpress.com or through e-mail links. A similar image, sometimes called a "Spotlight Tag," is used on americanexpress.com Web pages where transactions take place. The Tag collects numeric information, such as the dollar amount of an online purchase, to help us understand usage of the site. We do not use any of these electronic images to collect personally identifiable information.

Information We Collect When You Register

When you become a registered user on our site, you provide us with personal information such as your e-mail address and your Card account number. Becoming a registered user enables you to review confidential account information for the service(s) that you are enrolled in, and perform other confidential transactions.

Information We Collect After You Have Registered

American Express collects the following information after you have registered with us for an online product or service:

1. Your usage of americanexpress.com.

2. Your usage of the American Express online service in which you are enrolled.

How We Use Personal Information

Once you've become a registered americanexpress.com user, we use this information to deliver products and services you enroll in, and to process transactions you conduct on our website. We also use it, together with information we have about you as an American Express customer, publicly available information, and preferences you indicate, to customize your online experience and to provide you with more relevant online and offline offers and updates.

How We Use Your E-mail Address

We may use your e-mail address to send you the following types of e-mail messages:

1. Occasional updates about our products and services as well as American Express marketing offers.

2. Regularly scheduled e-mail newsletters related to the American Express products or services you are enrolled in.

3. Valuable offers from our business partners that we send you on their behalf. For examples of these offers, please visit the American Express Offer ZoneSM.

4. Service notifications related to your account(s).

You can also signup to receive the following types of e-mail messages from us:

1. Optional American Express e-mail newsletters. We occasionally invite customers to signup for these newsletters via email or other communications, and we also post signup forms on the American Express site.

2. American Express e-mail services. For example, registering to manage your Card accounts on our site includes an option to receive e-mail notifications when your monthly statements are available to view online.

You may decline to receive e-mail offers from American Express at any time.

We do not share your e-mail address with other companies for them to market their products or services to you. When we hire vendors to deliver e-mails to you on our behalf, they cannot use your e-mail address for any other purpose.

To make our e-mail offers more relevant to you, we may use information you provided in your initial transaction with us, in surveys, from information we have about you as an American Express customer—such as purchasing preferences or lifestyle—and information available from external sources such as census bureau data.

When we send e-mail to you, we may be able to identify information about your e-mail address, such as whether you can view graphic-rich HTML e-mail. If your e-mail address is HTML-enabled, we may choose to send you graphic-rich HTML e-mail messages.

These e-mail messages may contain "clear GIFs" or "Web beacons" to measure the offer's effectiveness so we know how to serve you better. We do not collect personally identifiable information through "clear GIFs" or "Web beacons."

You may also receive e-mail offers from another company for American Express products and services if you have actively requested that the company send you offers from its partners and/or advertisers. American Express does not provide these companies with personal information about you. To decline offers from other companies who may send offers on our behalf, follow the instructions provided by that company.

Setting Your Cookie Preferences

You can adjust your computer browser settings so that you are informed when a cookie is being placed in your browser. You can also set your browser to decline or accept all cookies. However, you must accept cookies if you need to access American Express site pages that enable you to review or use your confidential account information. These cookies are essential for site administration and security. Click here to learn more about setting your cookie preferences.

Ads That Link to Our Web Site

American Express hires other companies to place our banner ads on other Web sites and to perform tracking and reporting activities ("third-party advertisement servers"). They do not collect personally identifiable information in doing this work for us, and we do not give any personally identifiable information to them.

Third-party advertisement servers are subject to their own privacy policies. If you would like more information about the privacy policies of these third-party advertisement servers, including information on how to opt out of their tracking methods, please click here to visit the Network Advertising Initiative Web site.

Children Under 13

We do not knowingly solicit data online from or market online to children under the age of 13.

How We Safeguard Information

SSL Technology and How You Benefit From It

American Express realizes how important security is to you, so we've taken a number of steps to enhance the protection of personal or confidential information sent to or from American Express over the Internet. This includes Card and other account information. First, we require that a "secure session" be established, using Secure Socket Layer (SSL) Technology. This is done any time you supply or access personal or confidential information in one of our secure online areas.

SSL technology creates a private conversation that only your computer and American Express systems can understand. The SSL technology encodes information as it is being sent over the Internet between your computer and American Express systems, helping to ensure that the transmitted information remains confidential.

The use of SSL requires two components: an SSL-compatible browser and a Web server to perform the "key-exchange" that establishes a secure connection to American Express Web server systems.

The Technological Requirements Needed To Benefit From SSL Technology

1.   A Compliant Browser

You will need a browser with SSL capabilities. Examples of SSL browsers include Netscape 2.0 and above, Microsoft's Internet Explorer 2.0 and above, and the Web browser for America Online version 3.0 for Windows and above. (Note that some older versions of browsers will not support SSL sessions).

In order to securely access your personal or confidential information via the Internet, we recommend you use the latest browser versions available. Accessing secure online areas with Netscape versions before 1.12 (Mac or Unix) or 1.22 (Windows) is prohibited due to security concerns.

2.   A Compliant Internet Service Provider

Nearly all Internet Service Providers (ISPs) automatically enable the SSL session described above. If you use your company's internal connection to access the Internet and you find you cannot access the American Express secure pages with an SSL browser described above, your company may be blocking access via a "firewall." Please speak to your firm's Internet access systems administrator for further details on your network's Internet access.

3.   Enabled Cookies

You also must have enabled cookies on your browser in order to access confidential information. If you have chosen to disable cookies on your browser, you will not be able to access confidential information.

User ID and Password

Many areas of the site require the use of a User ID and Password as an additional security measure that helps protect your confidential information. This allows American Express to verify who you are, thereby allowing you access to your account information, and preventing unauthorized access.

When you have finished using a secure area of American Express Online Services, make sure you always click on the red "Exit Secure Area" or "Log Out" link which appears on the left-hand side of every secure page. When you click on it, you will be given the option to end your secure session. No further secure transactions can be conducted without re-entering your User ID and Password.

You should be aware that browser software often "caches" a page as you look at it, meaning that some pages are saved in your computer's temporary memory. Therefore, you may find that clicking on your "Back" button shows you a saved version of a previously viewed page. Caching in no way affects the security of your confidential User ID or Password. If you use a computer in a public place to access your account information, simply quit/exit the browser software before leaving to minimize the possibility of anyone else viewing your confidential information.

Selected Business Partners

In order to bring you the many online products and services offered by American Express, we work with carefully selected vendors and business partners. If we have to share any information with these companies in order to provide a product or service to you, we first conduct a careful evaluation of their information and security systems and practices, and require administrative, technical, and physical safeguards to ensure the security and confidentiality of American Express customer information. At any time, we may audit our partners and vendors to verify the continued security of their systems and practices.

Linking to Other Internet Sites

You should be aware that other Internet sites that you link to from the American Express site or an American Express e-mail may contain privacy provisions that differ from the provisions of our Privacy Statement. To ensure your privacy is protected, we recommend that you review the privacy statements of other Internet sites you visit.

How to Opt Out of E-mail Marketing Offers

To opt out of receiving e-mail offers or newsletters, click here. All e-mail offers and e-mail newsletters sent to you by American Express provide instructions on how to opt out of receiving future offers or newsletters. These instructions are located at the bottom of the e-mail message. You may receive separate newsletters pertaining to different American Express products and services. In that case, you must reply to and decline the newsletters individually. If you opt out, we will still send you e-mail with service updates as well as other important information related to the American Express online products or services for which you have signed up.

Your Other Opt-Out Choices

The American Express businesses that offer personal financial products also offer additional opt-out choices to their customers.

If you are enrolled in one or more of these American Express personal financial products, please call the Customer Service number on your account statement, or refer to the contact list below, to learn more about your opt-out choices.

1. American Express personal Card accounts: 1-800-528-4800

2. American Express Brokerage accounts: 1-800-297-7378

3. Membership Banking: 1-888-356-1006

4. American Express ONE Financial Account: 1-800-297-7378

Protecting Your Personal Information

Below is a helpful guide on the many ways you can protect your privacy. You can find out how companies collect, store, and use data related to your personal and financial history. You also have control over how certain information is used.

Private Payments

The Private Payments service from American Express offers privacy features that enhance and protect your online shopping experience. When you are ready to make an online purchase at any site that accepts the American Express Card, Private Payments will provide a randomly generated unique number and an associated expiration date in place of your actual American Express Card account number and expiration date.

When you register for Private Payments, we verify that you have an American Express Card registered for American Express online services. If you have not previously enrolled your American Express Card in our online services, you will be asked to register your American Express Card by providing your name, account number, and additional information to enable us to verify your identity.

We do not use any information you supply to us for Private Payments for any purpose other than the completion of your online purchase transactions and billing of your American Express Card. We will not share this information with any other parties, including any Web sites at which you may shop.

Credit Records

Credit bureaus compile records of individual consumers' credit habits to assist lenders, employers, and other businesses in assessing an applicant's creditworthiness. It is recommended that you obtain a copy of your credit report at least once a year to check for inaccuracies. Checking for inaccuracies will enable you to correct mistakes before you apply for a job, credit card, a loan, or insurance.

In the United States, credit records are usually maintained by credit bureaus that generally operate on one of three national reporting systems:

Equifax, Inc.

P.O. Box 740241
Atlanta, GA 30374-0241
800-685-1111
www.equifax.com

Experian, Inc. (formerly TRW)

P.O. Box 2002
Allen, TX 75013
888-397-3742
www.experian.com

Trans Union LLC

P.O. Box 1000
Chester, PA 19022
800-888-4213
www.transunion.com

Contact these bureaus for a copy of your credit report. Some bureaus charge a small fee for a copy of your report. The law requires that if you have been denied credit within the last 60 days, the bureau that supplied the report to the creditor must provide the report to you free of charge.

If you find inaccuracies or information that you want to clarify, contact the credit bureau and explain the error(s). The bureau is required to re-verify the information within 30 days or remove it from your file. If there is negative information that must remain in your file, you may provide the bureau with a brief explanation (100 words) that will be kept in your file. Negative information is generally kept for seven years; bankruptcy information for 10.

Telecommunications

Caller ID is a service offered by telephone companies in most areas across the United States. Subscribing to Caller ID allows you to see the numbers from which incoming calls are placed before you pick up the telephone. If you don't recognize a number, you have the choice to answer or not.

If you don't want your number revealed to those who have Caller ID, your local telephone company may offer per-call or per-line blocking mechanisms to prevent it from being displayed.

Companies with 800 and 900 numbers can use a similar identification technology to record your telephone number when you call. Some firms use your number to help retrieve your records faster and improve the quality and speed of handling your call. Be aware that some firms may also match your number to your name and address to add to customer lists created for marketing or service purposes.

Cellular and cordless phone conversations are easily monitored. You may choose to avoid conducting confidential conversations on these phones, especially phone calls in which you reveal credit card numbers or other personal or confidential information.

Rebate, Incentive, Discount, and Warranty Programs

Retailers that offer rebate and incentive programs often ask for your name, address, and phone number. If this concerns you, ask whether you can participate without providing this personal information.

Some retailers may provide you with a postcard or coupon offering a discount on their products or services. By redeeming the offer when you present the postcard or coupon, you may also be providing personal information to the retailer. This information may be used by the retailer to send you future marketing offers.

It is in your interest to return warranty cards to manufacturers with your contact information, so they can notify you about product warnings and recalls. You may leave blank those questions you feel are unnecessary, and request in writing to opt out of marketing programs based on the type of personal information you provide.

You may also want to contact the retailer to find out who has access to the information you are providing to them to participate in these programs. Some companies use this data to create mailing lists that are sold to marketers. Many consumers find receiving such offers a benefit; others do not.

Direct Mail, Telemarketing, and E-mail Offers

Many companies use direct mail, telemarketing, and e-mail to reach consumers. If you do not wish to be solicited, there are some steps you can take to reduce the number of solicitations you receive:

1. Write to the companies that are contacting you and ask to be removed from their lists.

2. Watch for special billing inserts provided by some companies that let you exclude your name from their lists.

3. Say "no" to telemarketers who want more information than you feel is necessary and to those who refuse to send follow-up explanatory materials. Under the Telephone Consumer Protection Act (a U.S. federal law), a telemarketer who calls you cannot continue this practice after you have requested that the calls stop.

4. Many states have their own laws and regulations governing telemarketing, and maintain "do not call" lists that you can sign up for. Check to see if your state has a "do not call" Web site.

5. Send an e-mail reply to the e-mails offers from companies or organizations you do not wish to hear from, and request to be removed from future e-mail marketing lists. Or, follow the opt-out instructions that the sender may provide in the e-mail offer.

6. Look for a privacy statement or policy on Web sites you visit. The statement should explain what information is collected, how it is used and safeguarded, and how to set your e-mail marketing preferences.

7. The Direct Marketing Association (DMA) maintains lists of consumers who do not wish to receive marketing offers by mail, e-mail, or phone. Registering for the DMA's Mail Preference Service, Email Preference Service, or Telephone Preference Service will help reduce the volume of offers you receive. Please note that the DMA charges consumers $5.00 to register online for these services. The DMA website is www.dmaconsumers.org/consumerassistance.html. The mailing addresses are as follows:

DMA Mail Preference Service
P.O. Box 643
Carmel, NY 1051⁄

or

DMA Telephone Preference Service
P.O. Box 1559
Carmel, NY 10512

Identification Needed for Purchases

When Paying With a Major Credit or Charge Card

1. Do not provide your telephone number for identification when using a major credit or charge card. However, a merchant that has no electronic or telephone connection with the card company to verify your account at the time of purchase may still ask for a telephone number.

2. Do not write your telephone number on credit or charge card purchase slips.

When Paying By Check

1. Do not put your Social Security number on your check.

2. Do not allow your credit or charge card account number to be written on your personal check. A number of states forbid merchants to record credit or charge card account numbers on personal checks. Merchants are permitted to simply note whether you have a major credit or charge card as an indicator of your creditworthiness. Exceptions include emergency check cashing, where you have pre-approved the use of your card to guarantee your check. Be forewarned, however, that merchants may refuse to accept your check if you refuse to allow them to record your card number.

For More Information

If you need further guidance, you may wish to consult the consumer affairs office of the company involved, the U.S. Better Business Bureau, or your local or state consumer protection agency.

Customer Privacy Principles

Because we strongly advocate the protection of customer information, we believe that the adoption and implementation of the following American Express Customer Privacy Principles makes good business sense and will serve the interests of our customers in effective privacy protection.

Our Customer Privacy Principles were first published in 1991, and they were modified in 1997. We are republishing these Principles now to reiterate our commitment and simplify the language.

These Customer Privacy Principles guide our conduct in the collection, use, release, and security of customer information. They outline the responsibilities we assume as employees and our expectations of business partners.

In working with our partners and vendors to identify customers and prospective customers for marketing purposes, we require strict contractual obligations regarding information use and security, including our right to audit those partners and vendors to ensure that they are adhering to our privacy requirements.

These Principles define our commitment to protect the privacy of our customers. Each American Express business unit may also maintain its own policies and practices, which are fully consistent with these Principles. In those jurisdictions that call for additional information practices, our policies and practices will meet the requirements of applicable law.

1. We collect only customer information that is needed, and we tell customers how we use it. We limit the collection of information about our customers to what we need to know to administer their accounts, to provide customer services, to offer new products and services, and to satisfy any legal and regulatory requirements. We also tell our customers about the general uses of information we collect about them, and we will provide additional explanation if customers request it.

2. We give customers choices about how their information will be used. Our businesses give customers "opt out" choices about how information about the customer's relationship with that business unit may be used to generate marketing offers. These marketing choices include product and service offers from American Express businesses and those made by our business partners. Of course, each of our businesses will continue to send its customers information relating to products or services they receive from that business.

3. We ensure information quality. We use advanced technology, documented procedures and internal monitoring practices to help ensure that customer information is processed promptly, accurately and completely. We will respond in a timely manner to customers' requests to correct inaccurate account or transaction information. We also require high standards of quality from the consumer reporting agencies and others that provide us with information about prospective customers.

4. We use prudent information security safeguards. We limit access to customer information systems to those who specifically need it to conduct their business responsibilities, and to meet our customer servicing commitments. We employ safeguards designed to protect the confidentiality and security of our customer information.

5. We limit the disclosure of customer information. We do not disclose customer information unless we have previously informed or been authorized by the customer, or we do so in connection with our efforts to reduce fraud or criminal activity and to comply with regulatory requirements and guidelines. When a court order or subpoena requires us to release information, we typically notify the customer to give the customer an opportu-

nity to exercise his or her legal rights. Further, we will not disclose or use health information for marketing purposes or use it as a basis to make credit decisions.

6. We are responsive to customers' requests for explanations. If we deny an application for our services or end a customer's relationship with us, to the extent permitted by applicable law, we will provide an explanation, if requested. We state the reasons for the action taken and the information upon which the decision was based, unless the issue involves potential criminal activity.

7. We hold ourselves responsible for our privacy principles. Each American Express employee is responsible for maintaining consumer confidence in the company. We provide training and communications programs designed to educate employees about the meaning and requirements of these Customer Privacy Principles. Employees who violate these Principles are subject to disciplinary action, up to and including dismissal. Employees are expected to report violations, and may do so confidentially, to their manager, to their business unit's compliance officer, or to the company's Office of the Ombudsperson.

8. We also conduct internal assessments of our privacy practices and periodically commission outside expert reviews of our compliance with the Privacy Principles and the specific policies and practices that support these Principles.

9. We extend these privacy principles to our business relationships. We require companies we select as our business partners to agree to keep our customer information confidential and secure, to protect the information against unauthorized access, use, or redisclosure by the recipient company, and limit its use to the purposes for which it was provided to them. We also encourage our business partners to respect their customers' information by adopting strong and effective privacy policies and practices, including offering "opt out" choices for marketing offers to their customers. In addition, we participate actively in industry associations to advocate development of comprehensive privacy policies and implementation strategies.

APPENDIX 17:
SAMPLE PRIVACY POLICY OUTLINE

1. IDENTITY OF THE WEB SITE ADMINISTRATORS

This is the Web site of [Company Name].

Our postal address is [Address].

We can be reached via e-mail at [e-mail address].

We can be reached by telephone at [telephone number].

2. FOR EACH VISITOR TO OUR WEB PAGE, OUR WEB SERVER AUTOMATICALLY RECOGNIZES: (CHOOSE ONE)

The consumer's domain name and e-mail address (where possible);

Only the consumer's domain name, but not the e-mail address (where possible);

No information regarding the domain or e-mail address; or

Other [please explain].

3. WE COLLECT: (CHOOSE ALL THAT APPLY)

Only the domain name, but not the e-mail address of visitors to our Web page;

The domain name and e-mail address (where possible) of visitors to our Web page;

The e-mail addresses of those who post messages to our bulletin board;

The e-mail addresses of those who communicate with us via e-mail;

The e-mail addresses of those who make postings to our chat areas;

Aggregate information on what pages consumers access or visit;

User-specific information on what pages consumers access or visit;

Information volunteered by the consumer, such as survey information and/or site registrations;

No information on consumers who browse our Web page; and/or

Other [please explain].

4. The information we collect is: (choose all that apply)

Used for internal review and is then discarded;

Used to improve the content of our Web page;

Used to customize the content and/or layout of our page for each individual visitor;

Used to notify visitors about updates to our Web site;

Used by us to contact consumers for marketing purposes;

Shared with other reputable organizations to help them contact consumers for marketing purposes;

Not shared with other organizations for commercial purposes; and/or

Other [please explain].

5. WITH RESPECT TO COOKIES:

We do not set any cookies; or

We use cookies to: (choose all that apply)

Store visitors preferences;

Record session information, such as items that consumers add to their shopping cart;

Record user-specific information on what pages users access or visit;

Alert visitors to new areas that we think might be of interest to them when they return to our site;

To record past activity at a site in order to provide better service when visitors return to our site;

Ensure that visitors are not repeatedly sent the same banner ads;

Customize Web page content on visitors' browser type or other information that the visitor sends; and/or

Other [please explain].

6. IF YOU DO NOT WANT TO RECEIVE E-MAIL FROM US IN THE FUTURE, PLEASE TELL US THAT YOU DO NOT WANT TO RECEIVE E-MAIL FROM OUR COMPANY AND PLEASE LET US KNOW BY: (CHOOSE ALL THAT APPLY)

Sending us e-mail at the above address;

Calling us at the above telephonc number;

Writing to us at the above address;

Visiting the following URL; and/or

Other [please explain].

7. FROM TIME TO TIME, WE MAKE THE E-MAIL ADDRESSES OF THOSE WHO ACCESS OUR SITE AVAILABLE TO OTHER REPUTABLE ORGANIZATIONS WHOSE PRODUCTS OR SERVICES WE THINK YOU MIGHT FIND INTERESTING. IF YOU DO NOT WANT US TO SHARE YOUR E-MAIL ADDRESS WITH OTHER COMPANIES OR ORGANIZATIONS, PLEASE TELL US THAT YOU DO NOT WANT US TO SHARE YOUR E-MAIL ADDRESS WITH OTHER COMPANIES, AND LET US KNOW BY: (CHOOSE ALL THAT APPLY)

Sending us e-mail at the above address;

Calling us at the above telephone number;

Writing to us at the above address;

Visiting the following URL; and/or

Other (please explain).

8. FROM TIME TO TIME, WE MAKE OUR CUSTOMER E-MAIL LIST AVAILABLE TO OTHER REPUTABLE ORGANIZATIONS WHOSE PRODUCTS OR SERVICES WE THINK YOU MIGHT FIND INTERESTING. IF YOU DO NOT WANT US TO SHARE YOUR E-MAIL ADDRESS WITH OTHER COMPANIES OR ORGANIZATIONS, PLEASE LET US KNOW BY: (CHOOSE ALL THAT APPLY)

Sending us e-mail at the above address;

Calling us at the above telephone number;

Writing to us at the above address;

Visiting the following URL; and/or

Other (please explain).

9. IF YOU SUPPLY US WITH YOUR POSTAL ADDRESS ONLINE: (CHOOSE EITHER OPTION 1 OR A COMBINATION OF OPTIONS 2 AND 3)

(1) you will only receive the information for which you provided us your address;

(2) you may receive periodic mailings from us with information on new products and services or upcoming events.

If you do not wish to receive such mailings, please let us know by: (choose all that apply)

Sending us e-mail at the above address;

Calling us at the above telephone number;

Writing to us at the above address;

Visiting the following URL; and/or

Other (please explain).

(3) you may receive mailings from other reputable companies. You can, however, have your name put on our do-not-share list by: (choose all that apply)

Sending us e-mail at the above address;

Calling us at the above telephone number;

Writing to us at the above address;

Visiting the following URL; and/or

Other (please explain).

Please provide us with your exact name and address. We will be sure your name is removed from the list we share with other organizations.

10. PERSONS WHO SUPPLY US WITH THEIR TELEPHONE NUMBERS ONLINE: (CHOOSE ALL THAT APPLY)

Will only receive telephone contact from us with information regarding orders they have placed online; and/or

May receive telephone contact from us with information regarding new products and services or upcoming events. If you do not wish to receive such telephone calls, please let us know by: (choose all that apply)

Sending us e-mail at the above address;

Calling us at the above telephone number;

Writing to us at the above address;

Visiting the following URL; and/or

Other (please explain)

May receive telephone contact from other reputable companies. You can, however, have your name put on our do-not-share list by: (choose all that apply)

Sending us e-mail at the above address;

Calling us at the above telephone number;

Writing to us at the above address;

Visiting the following URL; and/or

Other (please explain)

Please provide us with your name and phone number. We will be sure your name is removed from the list we share with other organizations.

11. AD SERVERS: (CHOOSE ONE)

We do not partner with or have special relationships with any ad server companies; or

To try and bring you offers that are of interest to you, we have relationships with other companies that we allow to place ads on our Web pages. As a result of your visit to our site, ad server companies may collect information such as your domain type, your IP address, and clickstream information. For further information, consult the privacy policies of:

[List the URLs for the privacy statements of the ad server companies with whom you have contracted or partnered].

12. FROM TIME TO TIME, WE MAY USE CUSTOMER INFORMATION FOR NEW, UNANTICIPATED USES NOT PREVIOUSLY DISCLOSED IN OUR PRIVACY NOTICE. IF OUR INFORMATION PRACTICES CHANGE AT SOME TIME IN THE FUTURE: (CHOOSE ALL THAT APPLY)

We will contact you before we use your data for these new purposes to notify you of the policy change and to provide you with the ability to opt out of these new uses;

We will post the policy changes to our Web site to notify you of these changes and provide you with the ability to opt out of these new uses. If you are concerned about how your information is used, you should check back at our Web site periodically;

We will use for these new purposes only data collected from the time of the policy change forward;

Customers may prevent their information from being used for purposes other than those for which it was originally collected by:

Sending us e-mail at the above address;

Calling us at the above telephone number;

Writing to us at the above address;

Visiting the following URL; or

Other (please explain).

13. UPON REQUEST WE PROVIDE SITE VISITORS WITH ACCESS TO: (CHOOSE ALL THAT APPLY)

All information [including proprietary information] that we maintain about them;

Financial information (e.g., credit card account information) that we maintain about them;

Unique identifier information (e.g., customer number or password) that we maintain about them;

Transaction information (e.g., dates on which customers made purchases, amounts and types of purchases) that we maintain about them;

Communications that the consumer/visitor has directed to our site (e.g., e-mails, customer inquiries);

Contact information (e.g., name, address, phone number) that we maintain about them;

A description of information that we maintain about them;

No information that we have collected and that we maintain about them;

Consumers can access this information by: (choose all that apply)

Sending us e-mail at the above address;

Calling us at the above telephone number;

Writing to us at the above address;

Visiting the following URL; and/or

Other (please explain).

14. UPON REQUEST WE OFFER VISITORS:

No ability to have factual inaccuracies corrected in information that we maintain about them; or

The ability to have inaccuracies corrected in: (choose all that apply)

Contact information;

Financial information;

Unique identifiers;

Transaction information;

Communications that the consumer/visitor has directed to the site; and/or

All information that we maintain.

Consumers can have this information corrected by: (choose all that apply)

Sending us e-mail at the above address;

Calling us at the above telephone number;

Writing to us at the above address;

Visiting the following URL; and/or

Other (please explain).

15. SECURITY: (CHOOSE ALL THAT APPLY)

We always use industry-standard encryption technologies when transferring and receiving consumer data exchanged with our site;

When we transfer and receive certain types of sensitive information such as financial or health information, we redirect visitors to a secure server and will notify visitors through a pop-up screen on our site;

We have appropriate security measures in place in our physical facilities to protect against the loss, misuse, or alteration of information that we have collected from you at our site; and/or

Other (please explain).

16. ENFORCEMENT:

If you feel that this site is not following its stated information policy, you may contact:

[Company Name] at the above addresses or phone number;

The DMA's Committee on Ethical Business Practices at mgoldberger@the-DMA.org;

State or local chapters of the Better Business Bureau;

State or local consumer protection office;

The Federal Trade Commission by telephone at: 202-FTC-HELP (202-382-4357); or electronically at http://www.ftc.gov/to/romap2.htm; and/or

Other [please explain].

Source: The Direct Marketing Association.

APPENDIX 18:
CODE OF INFORMATION PRACTICES

1. There must be no personal data record-keeping systems whose very existence is secret.

2. There must be a way for a user to find out what personal information has been recorded and how it is used.

3. There must be a way for a user to prevent a site or company from using personal information for any reason other than its original intent.

4. There must be a way for a user to correct or amend a record of identifiable information about the person.

5. Any entity creating, maintaining, using or disseminating records of identifiable personal data must assure the reliability of the data for their intended use and must take precautions to prevent misuses of the data.

Source: U.S. Department of Health, Education and Welfare, Secretary's Advisory Committee on Automated Personal Data Systems, Records, Computers, and the Rights of Citizens.

APPENDIX 19:
THE SAFEGUARDS RULE

FEDERAL TRADE COMMISSION [16 CFR PART 314]

PART 314–STANDARDS FOR SAFEGUARDING CUSTOMER INFORMATION

§ 314.1 Purpose and scope.

(a) Purpose. This part ("rule"), which implements sections 501 and 505(b)(2) of the Gramm-Leach-Bliley Act, sets forth standards for developing, implementing, and maintaining reasonable administrative, technical, and physical safeguards to protect the security, confidentiality, and integrity of customer information.

(b) Scope. This rule applies to the handling of customer information by all financial institutions over which the Federal Trade Commission ("FTC" or "Commission") has jurisdiction. This rule refers to such entities as "you." The rule applies to all customer information in your possession, regardless of whether such information pertains to individuals with whom you have a customer relationship, or pertains to the customers of other financial institutions that have provided such information to you.

§ 314.2 Definitions.

(a) In general. Except as modified by this rule or unless the context otherwise requires, the terms used in this rule have the same meaning as set forth in the Commission's rule governing the Privacy of Consumer Financial Information, 16 CFR part 313.

(b) "Customer information" means any record containing nonpublic personal information as defined in 16 CFR 313.3(n), about a customer of a financial institution, whether in paper, electronic, or other form, that is handled or maintained by or on behalf of you or your affiliates.

(c) "Information security program" means the administrative, technical, or physical safeguards you use to access, collect, distribute, process, protect, store, use, transmit, dispose of, or otherwise handle customer information.

(d) "Service provider" means any person or entity that receives, maintains, processes, or otherwise is permitted access to customer information through its provision of services directly to a financial institution that is subject to the rule.

§ 314.3 Standards for safeguarding customer information.

(a) Information security program. You shall develop, implement, and maintain a comprehensive information security program that is written in one or more readily accessible parts and contains administrative, technical, and physical safeguards that are appropriate to your size and complexity, the nature and scope of your activities, and the sensitivity of any customer information at issue. Such safeguards shall include the elements set forth in section 314.4 and shall be reasonably designed to achieve the objectives of this rule, as set forth in paragraph (b) of this section.

(b) Objectives. The objectives of section 501(b) of the Act, and of this rule, are to:

(1) Insure the security and confidentiality of customer information;

(2) Protect against any anticipated threats or hazards to the security or integrity of such information; and

(3) Protect against unauthorized access to or use of such information that could result in substantial harm or inconvenience to any customer.

§ 314.4 Elements.

In order to develop, implement, and maintain your information security program, you shall:

(a) Designate an employee or employees to coordinate your information security program.

(b) Identify reasonably foreseeable internal and external risks to the security, confidentiality, and integrity of customer information that could result in the unauthorized disclosure, misuse, alteration, destruction or other compromise of such information, and assess the sufficiency of any safeguards in place to control these risks. At a minimum, such a risk assessment should include consideration of risks in each relevant area of your operations, including:

(1) employee training and management;

(2) information systems, including network and software design, as well as information processing, storage, transmission and disposal; and

(3) detecting, preventing and responding to attacks, intrusions, or other systems failures.

(c) Design and implement information safeguards to control the risks you identify through risk assessment, and regularly test or otherwise monitor the effectiveness of the safeguards' key controls, systems, and procedures.

(d) Oversee service providers, by:

(1) taking reasonable steps to select and retain service providers that are capable of maintaining appropriate safeguards for the customer information at issue; and

(2) requiring your service providers by contract to implement and maintain such safeguards.

(e) Evaluate and adjust your information security program in light of the results of the testing and monitoring required by paragraph (c); any material changes to your operations or business arrangements; or any other circumstances that you know or have reason to know may have a material impact on your information security program.

§ 314.5 Effective date.

(a) Each financial institution subject to the Commission's jurisdiction must implement an information security program pursuant to this rule no later than one year from the date on which the Final Rule is published in the Federal Register.

(b) Two-year grandfathering of service contracts. Until two years from the date on which the Final Rule is published in the Federal Register, a contract you have entered into with a nonaffiliated third party to perform services for you or functions on your behalf satisfies the provisions of section 314.4(d) of this part, even if the contract does not include a requirement that the service provider maintain appropriate safeguards, as long as you entered into the contract not later than 30 days from the date on which the Final Rule is published in the Federal Register.

By direction of the Commission.

Donald S. Clark Secretary

APPENDIX 20:
THE CHILDREN'S ONLINE PRIVACY PROTECTION ACT (COPPA)

SEC. 1301. SHORT TITLE.

This title may be cited as the "Children's Online Privacy Protection Act of 1998". SEC. 1302. DEFINITIONS.

In this title:

(1) CHILD.—The term "child" means an individual under the age of 13.

(2) OPERATOR.—The term "operator"—

(A) means any person who operates a website located on the Internet or an online service and who collects or maintains personal information from or about the users of or visitors to such website or online service, or on whose behalf such information is collected or maintained, where such website or online service is operated for commercial purposes, including any person offering products or services for sale through that website or online service, involving commerce—

(i) among the several States or with 1 or more foreign nations;

(ii) in any territory of the United States or in the District of Columbia, or between any such territory and—

(I) another such territory; or

(II) any State or foreign nation; or

(iii) between the District of Columbia and any State, territory, or foreign nation; but

(B) does not include any nonprofit entity that would otherwise be exempt from coverage under section 5 of the Federal Trade Commission Act (15 U.S.C. 45).

(3) COMMISSION.—The term "Commission" means the Federal Trade Commission.

(4) DISCLOSURE.—The term "disclosure" means, with respect to personal information—

(A) the release of personal information collected from a child in identifiable form by an operator for any purpose, except where such information is provided to a person other than the operator who provides support for the internal operations of the website and does not disclose or use that information for any other purpose; and

(B) making personal information collected from a child by a website or online service directed to children or with actual knowledge that such information was collected from a child, publicly available in identifiable form, by any means including by a public posting, through the Internet, or through—

(i) a home page of a website;

(ii) a pen pal service;

(iii) an electronic mail service;

(iv) a message board; or

(v) a chat room.

(5) FEDERAL AGENCY.—The term "Federal agency" means an agency, as that term is defined in section 551(1) of title 5, United States Code.

(6) INTERNET.—The term "Internet" means collectively the myriad of computer and telecommunications facilities, including equipment and operating software, which comprise the interconnected world-wide network of networks that employ the Transmission Control Protocol/Internet Protocol, or any predecessor or successor protocols to such protocol, to communicate information of all kinds by wire or radio.

(7) PARENT.—The term "parent" includes a legal guardian.

(8) PERSONAL INFORMATION.—The term "personal information" means individually identifiable information about an individual collected online, including—

(A) a first and last name;

(B) a home or other physical address including street name and name of a city or town;

(C) an e-mail address;

(D) a telephone number;

(E) a Social Security number;

(F) any other identifier that the Commission determines permits the physical or online contacting of a specific individual; or

(G) information concerning the child or the parents of that child that the website collects online from the child and combines with an identifier described in this paragraph.

(9) VERIFIABLE PARENTAL CONSENT.—The term "verifiable parental consent" means any reasonable effort (taking into consideration available technology), including a request for authorization for future collection, use, and disclosure described in the notice, to ensure that a parent of a child receives notice of the operator's personal information collection, use, and disclosure practices, and authorizes the collection, use, and disclosure, as applicable, of personal information and the subsequent use of that information before that information is collected from that child.

(10) WEBSITE OR ONLINE SERVICE DIRECTED TO CHILDREN.—

(A) IN GENERAL.—The term "website or online service directed to children" means—

(i) a commercial website or online service that is targeted to children; or

(ii) that portion of a commercial website or online service that is targeted to children.

(B) LIMITATION.—A commercial website or online service, or a portion of a commercial website or online service, shall not be deemed directed to children solely for referring or linking to a commercial website or online service directed to children by using information location tools, including a directory, index, reference, pointer, or hypertext link.

(11) PERSON.—The term "person" means any individual, partnership, corporation, trust, estate, cooperative, association, or other entity.

(12) ONLINE CONTACT INFORMATION.—The term "online contact information" means an e-mail address or an-other substantially similar identifier that permits direct contact with a person online.

SEC. 1303. REGULATION OF UNFAIR AND DECEPTIVE ACTS AND PRACTICES IN CONNECTION WITH THE COLLECTION AND USE OF PERSONAL INFORMATION FROM AND ABOUT CHILDREN ON THE INTERNET.

(a) ACTS PROHIBITED.—

(1) IN GENERAL.—It is unlawful for an operator of a website or online service directed to children, or any operator that has actual knowledge

that it is collecting personal information from a child, to collect personal information from a child in a manner that violates the regulations prescribed under subsection (b).

(2) DISCLOSURE TO PARENT PROTECTED.—Notwithstanding paragraph (1), neither an operator of such a website or online service nor the operator's agent shall be held to be liable under any Federal or State law for any disclosure made in good faith and following reasonable procedures in responding to a request for disclosure of personal information under subsection (b)(1)(B)(iii) to the parent of a child.

(b) REGULATIONS.—

(1) IN GENERAL.—Not later than 1 year after the date of the enactment of this Act, the Commission shall promulgate under section 553 of title 5, United States Code, regulations that—

(A) require the operator of any website or online service directed to children that collects personal information from children or the operator of a website or online service that has actual knowledge that it is collecting personal information from a child—

(i) to provide notice on the website of what information is collected from children by the operator, how the operator uses such information, and the operator's disclosure practices for such information; and

(ii) to obtain verifiable parental consent for the collection, use, or disclosure of personal information from children;

(B) require the operator to provide, upon request of a parent under this subparagraph whose child has provided personal information to that website or online service, upon proper identification of that parent, to such parent—

(i) a description of the specific types of personal information collected from the child by that operator;

(ii) the opportunity at any time to refuse to permit the operator's further use or maintenance in retrievable form, or future online collection, of personal information from that child; and

(iii) notwithstanding any other provision of law, a means that is reasonable under the circumstances for the parent to obtain any personal information collected from that child;

(C) prohibit conditioning a child's participation in a game, the offering of a prize, or another activity on the child disclosing more personal information than is reasonably necessary to participate in such activity; and

(D) require the operator of such a website or online service to establish and maintain reasonable procedures to protect the confidentiality, security, and integrity of personal information collected from children.

(2) WHEN CONSENT NOT REQUIRED.—The regulations shall provide that verifiable parental consent under paragraph (1)(A)(ii) is not required in the case of—

(A) online contact information collected from a child that is used only to respond directly on a one-time basis to a specific request from the child and is not used to recontact the child and is not maintained in retrievable form by the operator;

(B) a request for the name or online contact information of a parent or child that is used for the sole purpose of obtaining parental consent or providing notice under this section and where such information is not maintained in retrievable form by the operator if parental consent is not obtained after a reasonable time;

(C) online contact information collected from a child that is used only to respond more than once directly to a specific request from the child and is not used to recontact the child beyond the scope of that request—

(i) if, before any additional response after the initial response to the child, the operator uses reasonable efforts to provide a parent notice of the online contact information collected from the child, the purposes for which it is to be used, and an opportunity for the parent to request that the operator make no further use of the information and that it not be maintained in retrievable form; or

(ii) without notice to the parent in such circumstances as the Commission may determine are appropriate, taking into consideration the benefits to the child of access to information and services, and risks to the security and privacy of the child, in regulations promulgated under this subsection;

(D) the name of the child and online contact information (to the extent reasonably necessary to protect the safety of a child participant on the site)—

(i) used only for the purpose of protecting such safety;

(ii) not used to recontact the child or for any other purpose; and

(iii) not disclosed on the site, if the operator uses reasonable efforts to provide a parent notice of the name and online contact information collected from the child, the purposes for which it is to be used, and an opportunity for the parent to request that the operator make no further use of the information and that it not be maintained in retrievable form; or

(E) the collection, use, or dissemination of such information by the operator of such a website or online service necessary—

(i) to protect the security or integrity of its website;

(ii) to take precautions against liability;

(iii) to respond to judicial process; or

(iv) to the extent permitted under other provisions of law, to provide information to law enforcement agencies or for an investigation on a matter related to public safety.

(3) TERMINATION OF SERVICE.—The regulations shall permit the operator of a website or an online service to terminate service provided to a child whose parent has refused, under the regulations prescribed under paragraph (1)(B)(ii), to permit the operator's further use or maintenance in retrievable form, or future online collection, of personal information from that child.

(c) ENFORCEMENT.—Subject to sections 1304 and 1306, a violation of a regulation prescribed under subsection (a) shall be treated as a violation of a rule defining an unfair or deceptive act or practice prescribed under section 18(a)(1)(B) of the Federal Trade Commission Act (15 U.S.C. 57a(a)(1)(B)).

(d) INCONSISTENT STATE LAW.—No State or local government may impose any liability for commercial activities or actions by operators in interstate or foreign commerce in connection with an activity or action described in this title that is inconsistent with the treatment of those activities or actions under this section.

SEC. 1304. SAFE HARBORS.

(a) GUIDELINES.—An operator may satisfy the requirements of regulations issued under section 1303(b) by following a set of self-regulatory guidelines, issued by representatives of the marketing or online industries, or by other persons, approved under subsection (b).

(b) INCENTIVES.—

(1) SELF-REGULATORY INCENTIVES.—In prescribing regulations under section 1303, the Commission shall provide incentives for self-regulation by operators to implement the protections afforded children

under the regulatory requirements described in subsection (b) of that section.

(2) DEEMED COMPLIANCE.—Such incentives shall include provisions for ensuring that a person will be deemed to be in compliance with the requirements of the regulations under section 1303 if that person complies with guidelines that, after notice and comment, are approved by the Commission upon making a determination that the guidelines meet the requirements of the regulations issued under section 1303.

(3) EXPEDITED RESPONSE TO REQUESTS.—The Commission shall act upon requests for safe harbor treatment within 180 days of the filing of the request, and shall set forth in writing its conclusions with regard to such requests.

(c) APPEALS.—Final action by the Commission on a request for approval of guidelines, or the failure to act within 180 days on a request for approval of guidelines, submitted under subsection (b) may be appealed to a district court of the United States of appropriate jurisdiction as provided for in section 706 of title 5, United States Code.

SEC. 1305. ACTIONS BY STATES.

(a) IN GENERAL.—

(1) CIVIL ACTIONS.—In any case in which the attorney general of a State has reason to believe that an interest of the residents of that State has been or is threatened or adversely affected by the engagement of any person in a practice that violates any regulation of the Commission prescribed under section 1303(b), the State, as parens patriae, may bring a civil action on behalf of the residents of the State in a district court of the United States of appropriate jurisdiction to—

(A) enjoin that practice;

(B) enforce compliance with the regulation;

(C) obtain damage, restitution, or other compensation on behalf of residents of the State; or

(D) obtain such other relief as the court may consider to be appropriate.

(2) NOTICE.—

(A) IN GENERAL.—Before filing an action under paragraph (1), the attorney general of the State involved shall provide to the Commission—

(i) written notice of that action; and

(ii) a copy of the complaint for that action.

(B) EXEMPTION.—

(i) IN GENERAL.—Subparagraph (A) shall not apply with respect to the filing of an action by an attorney general of a State under this subsection, if the attorney general determines that it is not feasible to provide the notice described in that subparagraph before the filing of the action.

(ii) NOTIFICATION.—In an action described in clause (i), the attorney general of a State shall provide notice and a copy of the complaint to the Commission at the same time as the attorney general files the action.

(b) INTERVENTION.—

(1) IN GENERAL.—On receiving notice under subsection (a)(2), the Commission shall have the right to intervene in the action that is the subject of the notice.

(2) EFFECT OF INTERVENTION.—If the Commission intervenes in an action under subsection (a), it shall have the right—

(A) to be heard with respect to any matter that arises in that action; and

(B) to file a petition for appeal.

(3) AMICUS CURIAE.—Upon application to the court, a person whose self-regulatory guidelines have been approved by the Commission and are relied upon as a defense by any defendant to a proceeding under this section may file amicus curiae in that proceeding.

(c) CONSTRUCTION.—For purposes of bringing any civil action under subsection (a), nothing in this title shall be construed to prevent an attorney general of a State from exercising the powers conferred on the attorney general by the laws of that State to—

(1) conduct investigations;

(2) administer oaths or affirmations; or

(3) compel the attendance of witnesses or the production of documentary and other evidence.

(d) ACTIONS BY THE COMMISSION.—In any case in which an action is instituted by or on behalf of the Commission for violation of any regulation prescribed under section 1303, no State may, during the pendency of that action, institute an action under subsection (a) against any defendant named in the complaint in that action for violation of that regulation.

(e) VENUE; SERVICE OF PROCESS.—

(1) VENUE.—Any action brought under subsection (a) may be brought in the district court of the United States that meets applicable requirements relating to venue under section 1391 of title 28, United States Code.

(2) SERVICE OF PROCESS.—In an action brought under subsection (a), process may be served in any district in which the defendant—

(A) is an inhabitant; or

(B) may be found.

SEC. 1306. ADMINISTRATION AND APPLICABILITY OF ACT.

(a) IN GENERAL.—Except as otherwise provided, this title shall be enforced by the Commission under the Federal Trade Commission Act (15 U.S.C. 41 et seq.).

(b) PROVISIONS.—Compliance with the requirements imposed under this title shall be enforced under—

(1) section 8 of the Federal Deposit Insurance Act (12 U.S.C. 1818), in the case of—

(A) national banks, and Federal branches and Federal agencies of foreign banks, by the Office of the Comptroller of the Currency;

(B) member banks of the Federal Reserve System (other than national banks), branches and agencies of foreign banks (other than Federal branches, Federal agencies, and insured State branches of foreign banks), commercial lending companies owned or controlled by foreign banks, and organizations operating under section 25 or 25(a) of the Federal Reserve Act (12 U.S.C. 601 et seq. and 611 et seq.), by the Board; and

(C) banks insured by the Federal Deposit Insurance Corporation (other than members of the Federal Reserve System) and insured State branches of foreign banks, by the Board of Directors of the Federal Deposit Insurance Corporation;

(2) section 8 of the Federal Deposit Insurance Act (12 U.S.C. 1818), by the Director of the Office of Thrift Supervision, in the case of a savings association the deposits of which are insured by the Federal Deposit Insurance Corporation;

(3) the Federal Credit Union Act (12 U.S.C. 1751 et seq.) by the National Credit Union Administration Board with respect to any Federal credit union;

(4) part A of subtitle VII of title 49, United States Code, by the Secretary of Transportation with respect to any air carrier or foreign air carrier subject to that part;

(5) the Packers and Stockyards Act, 1921 (7 U.S.C. 181 et seq.) (except as provided in section 406 of that Act (7 U.S.C. 226, 227)), by the Secretary of Agriculture with respect to any activities subject to that Act; and

(6) the Farm Credit Act of 1971 (12 U.S.C. 2001 et seq.) by the Farm Credit Administration with respect to any Federal land bank, Federal land bank association, Federal intermediate credit bank, or production credit association.

(c) EXERCISE OF CERTAIN POWERS.—For the purpose of the exercise by any agency referred to in subsection (a) of its powers under any Act referred to in that subsection, a violation of any requirement imposed under this title shall be deemed to be a violation of a requirement imposed under that Act. In addition to its powers under any provision of law specifically referred to in subsection (a), each of the agencies referred to in that subsection may exercise, for the purpose of enforcing compliance with any requirement imposed under this title, any other authority conferred on it by law.

(d) ACTIONS BY THE COMMISSION.—The Commission shall prevent any person from violating a rule of the Commission under section 1303 in the same manner, by the same means, and with the same jurisdiction, powers, and duties as though all applicable terms and provisions of the Federal Trade Commission Act (15 U.S.C. 41 et seq.) were incorporated into and made a part of this title. Any entity that violates such rule shall be subject to the penalties and entitled to the privileges and immunities provided in the Federal Trade Commission Act in the same manner, by the same means, and with the same jurisdiction, power, and duties as though all applicable terms and provisions of the Federal Trade Commission Act were incorporated into and made a part of this title.

(e) EFFECT ON OTHER LAWS.—Nothing contained in the Act shall be construed to limit the authority of the Commission under any other provisions of law.

SEC. 1307. REVIEW.

Not later than 5 years after the effective date of the regulations initially issued under section 1303, the Commission shall—

(1) review the implementation of this title, including the effect of the implementation of this title on practices relating to the collection and disclosure of information relating to children, children's ability to ob-

tain access to information of their choice online, and on the availability of websites directed to children; and

(2) prepare and submit to Congress a report on the results of the review under paragraph (1).

SEC. 1308. EFFECTIVE DATE. SECTIONS 1303(A), 1305, AND 1306 OF THIS TITLE TAKE EFFECT ON THE LATER OF—

(1) the date that is 18 months after the date of enactment of this Act; or

(2) the date on which the Commission rules on the first application filed for safe harbor treatment under section 1304 if the Commission does not rule on the first such application within one year after the date of enactment of this Act, but in no case later than the date that is 30 months after the date of enactment of this Act.

GLOSSARY

Ad Blocker—Software placed on a user's personal computer that prevents advertisements from being displayed on the Web.

Ad Network—Companies that purchase and place banner advertisements on behalf of their clients.

Affirmative Customization—Refers to a site's or an Internet service provider's use of personal data to tailor or modify the content or design of the site to specifications affirmatively selected by a particular individual.

Aggregate Information—Information that is related to a website visitor but is not about that individually personally, e.g., information kept about which pages on a website are most popular to a visitor but which cannot be traced to the individual personally.

Anonymity—A situation in which the user's true identity is not known.

Anonymizer—A service that prevents Web sites from seeing a user's Internet Protocol (IP) address. The service operates as an intermediary to protect the user's identity.

Anonymous Remailer—A special e-mail server that acts as a middleman and strips outgoing e-mail of all personally identifying information, then forwards it to its destination, usually with the IP address of the remailer attached.

Authenticate—Process of verifying that the person attempting to send a message or access data is who he or she claims to be.

Authorize—To grant or deny a person access to data or systems.

Bankrupt—Bankrupt refers to the state or condition of one who is unable to pay his debts as they are, or become, due.

Bankruptcy—Bankruptcy is the legal process under federal law intended to insure fairness and equality among creditors of a bankrupt person, also known as a debtor, and to enable the debtor to start fresh by retaining certain property exempt from liabilities and unhampered by preexisting debts.

Banner Ad—Advertisement for a product or company that is placed on a Web page in order to sell site visitors a good or service. Clicking on a banner will take the visitor to a site to learn more about that product or service.

BBBOnline—Refers to the Better Business Bureau's Online privacy seal program. BBBOnline certifies sites that meet baseline privacy standards. The program requires its licensees to implement certain fair information practices and to submit to various types of compliance monitoring in order to display a privacy seal on their websites.

Blocking Software—A computer program that allows parents, teachers, or guardians to "block" access to certain websites and other information available over the Internet.

Bookmark—A bookmark is an online function that lets the user access their favorite web sites quickly.

Browser—A browser is special software that allows the user to navigate several areas of the internet and view a website.

Bulletin Board—A bulletin board is a place to leave an electronic message or share news to which anyone can read and reply.

Cache—A cache is a place on the computer's hard drive where the browser stores information from pages or sites that the user has visited so that returning to those pages or sites is faster and easier.

Chat Room—A chat room is a place for people to converse online by typing messages to each other.

Chatting—Chatting is a way for a group of people to converse online in real-time by typing messages to each other.

Children's Online Privacy Protection Act (COPPA)—Law that prescribes a set of rules meant to protect children's privacy online.

Ciphertext—Scrambled, unreadable contents of an encrypted message or file.

Common Law—Common law is the system of jurisprudence which originated in England and was later applied in the United States. The common law is based on judicial precedent rather than statutory law.

Compensatory Damages—Compensatory damages are those damages directly referable to the breach or tortious act and which can be readily proven to have been sustained and for which the injured party should be compensated as a matter of right. Also referred to as actual or general damages.

Consent—Explicit permission, given to a website by a visitor, to handle personal information in specified ways. "Informed consent" implies that the company fully discloses its information practices prior to obtaining personal data or permission to use it.

Consequential Damages—Consequential damages are those damages which are caused by an injury but which are not a necessary result of the injury and must be specially pleaded and proven in order to be awarded.

Cookie—When the user visits a site, a notation may be fed to a file known as a "cookie" in their computer for future reference. If the user revisits the site, the "cookie" file allows the web site to identify the user as a "return" guest and offers the user products tailored to their interests or tastes.

Cookie Buster—Software that is designed to block the placement of cookies by ad networks and Web sites thus preventing companies from tracking a user's activity.

Credit—Credit is that which is extended to the buyer or borrower on the seller or lender's belief that that which is given will be repaid.

Credit Report—A credit report refers to the document from a credit reporting agency setting forth a credit rating and pertinent financial data concerning a person or a company, which is used by banks, lenders, merchants, and suppliers in evaluating a credit risk.

Criminal Impersonation—As it pertains to identity theft, means to knowingly assume a false or fictitious identity or capacity, and in that identity or capacity, doing any act with intent to unlawfully gain a benefit or injure or defraud another.

Cyberspace—Cyberspace is another name for the internet.

Damages—In general, damages refers to monetary compensation which the law awards to one who has been injured by the actions of another, such as in the case of tortious conduct or breach of contractual obligations.

Data Spill—The result of a poorly designed form on a website which may cause an information leak to web servers of other companies, such as an ad network or advertising agency.

Decrypt—To decode data from its protected, scrambled form so it can be read.

Digital Certificate—Process using encryption technology whereby a document can be digitally stamped or certified as to its place of origin, and a certification authority supports and legitimizes the certificates.

Digital Signature—A digital signature is a digital certification or stamp that uses encryption technology to authenticate an individual's signature is legitimate.

Digital storm—Analytic tools currently being developed by the FBI to sift and link data from disparate sources.

Directories—Indexes of web pages organized by subject.

Disclosure—Disclosure is the act of disclosing or revealing that which is secret or not fully understood. The Truth in Lending Act provides that there be disclosure to the consumer of certain information deemed basic to an intelligent assessment of a credit transaction.

Download—A download is the transfer of files or software from a remote computer to the user's computer.

Downstream Data Use—Refers to companies' practice of disclosing personal information collected from users to other parties downstream to facilitate a transaction.

Dynamic IP Address—An IP address that changes every time a user logs on, or dials-up, to a computer.

Encryption—The scrambling of digital information so that it is unreadable to the average user. A computer must have "digital keys" to unscramble and read the information.

Encryption Software—Often used as a security measure, encryption software scrambles data so that it is unreadable to interceptors without the appropriate information to read the data.

E-Mail—E-mail is computer-to-computer messages between one or more individuals via the Internet.

Ethernet—A commonly used networking technology that links computers together.

Ethernet Adapter Address—The personal name of the Ethernet card in a user's computer.

Federal Trade Commission—The Federal Trade Commission is an agency of the federal government created in 1914 for the purpose of promoting free and fair competition in interstate commerce through the prevention of general trade restraints such as price-fixing agreements, false advertising, boycotts, illegal combinations of competitors and other unfair methods of competition.

File Transfer Protocol (FTP)—A way to transfer files from one computer to another.

Filter—Filter is software the user can buy that lets the user block access to websites and content that they may find unsuitable.

Finance Charge—A finance charge is any charge assessed for an extension of credit, including interest.

Financial Information—Refers to information identifiable to an individual that concerns the amount and conditions of an individual's assets, liabilities, or credit, including (a) Account numbers and balances; (b) Transactional information concerning an account; and (c) Codes, passwords, social security numbers, tax identification numbers, driver's license or permit numbers, state identification numbers and other information held for the purpose of account access or transaction initiation.

Financial Information Repository—Refers to a person engaged in the business of providing services to customers who have a credit, deposit, trust, stock, or other financial account or relationship with the person.

Firewall—A hardware or software device that controls access to computers on a Local Area Network (LAN). It examines all traffic routed between the two networks—inbound and outbound—to see if it meets certain criteria. If it does it is routed between the networks, otherwise it is stopped. It can also manage public access to private networked resources such as host applications.

Fraud—Fraud is a false representation of a matter of fact, whether by words or by conduct, by false or misleading allegations, or by concealment of that which should have been disclosed, which deceives and is intended to deceive another so that he shall act upon it to his legal injury.

General Damages—General damages are those damages directly referable to the breach or tortious act and which can be readily proven to have been sustained and for which the injured party should be compensated as a matter of right. Also referred to as actual or compensatory damages.

Grace Period—The grace period is the period beyond the due date set forth in the contract during which time payment may be made without incurring a penalty.

Globally Unique Identifier (GUID)—a unique code used to identify a computer, user, file, etc., for tracking purposes.

Hardware—The computer and related machines such as scanners and printers.

Host Name—Each computer is given a name which typically includes the user name and the organizational owner of the computer.

Home Page—The first page or document web users see when connecting to a web server or when visiting a website.

Hyperlink—An image or portion of text on a web page that is linked to another web page The user clicks on the link to go to another web page or another place on the same page.

Hypertext Markup Language (HTML)—The standard language used for creating documents on the Internet.

Hypertext Transfer Protocol (HTTP)—The standard language that computers connected to the Internet use to communicate with each other.

Impossibility—Impossibility is a defense to breach of contract and arises when performance is impossible due to the destruction of the subject matter of the contract or the death of a person necessary for performance.

Indemnification Clause—An indemnification clause in a contract refers to the agreement by one party to secure the other party against loss or damage which may occur in the future in connection with performance of the contract.

Installment Contract—An installment contract is one in which the obligation, such as the payment of money, is divided into a series of successive performances over a period of time loaned.

Instant Message—A chat-like technology on an online service that notifies a user when another is online, allowing for simultaneous communication.

Interest—Interest is the compensation paid for the use of money

Internal Protocol (IP)—The standards by which computers talk to each other over the Internet.

Internet—The internet is the universal network that allows computers to talk to other computers in words, text, graphics, and sound, anywhere in the world.

Internet Service Provider (ISP)—A service that allows the user to connect to the internet.

IP Address—A number or series of numbers that identify a computer linked to the Internet and which is generally written as four numbers separated by periods, e.g. 12.24.36.48.

JavaScript—A programming language used to add features to web pages in order to make the website more interactive.

Joint and Several—Joint and several refers to the sharing of rights and liabilities among a group of people collectively and individually.

Judgment—A judgment is a final determination by a court of law concerning the rights of the parties to a lawsuit.

Junk E-mail—Junk e-mail is unsolicited commercial e-mail also known as "spam."

Keyword—A keyword is a word the user enters into a search engine to begin the search for specific information or websites.

Liability—Liability refers to one's obligation to do or refrain from doing something, such as the payment of a debt.

Links—Links are highlighted words on a website that allow the user to connect to other parts of the same website or to other websites.

Listserve—Listserve is an online mailing list that allows individuals or organizations to send e-mail to groups of people at one time.

Local Area Network (LAN)—A computer network limited to the immediate area, usually the same building or floor of a building.

Means of Identification—As it pertains to identity theft, refers to any name or number that may be used, alone or in conjunction with any other information, to identify a specific individual, including a current or former name of the person, telephone number, an electronic address, or identifier of the individual or a member of his or her family, including the ancestor of the person; information relating to a change in name, address, telephone number, or electronic address or identifier of the individual or his or her family; a social security, driver's license, or tax identification number of the individual or a member of his or her family; and other information that could be used to identify the person, including unique biometric data.

Media Access Control—The unique Ethernet card ID number found in network computers.

Modem—a modem is an internal or external device that connects the computer to a phone line and, if the user wishes, to a company that can link the user to the internet.

Mouse—A small device attached to the computer by a cord, which lets the user give commands to the computer by clicking.

Online profiling—The practice of aggregating information about consumers' preferences and interests, gathered primarily by tracking their online movements and actions, with the purpose of creating targeted advertisement using the resulting profiles.

Online Service—An online service is an ISP with added information, entertainment and shopping features.

Operating system—The main program that runs on a computer.

Operator—The person who is responsible for maintaining and running a website.

Opt-In—Refers to when a user gives explicit permission for a company to use personal information for marketing purposes.

Opt-Out—Refers to when a user prohibits a company from using personal information for marketing purposes.

Packet—Term for the small bundles of digital information passed between users and sites.

Packet Sniffer—A software tool used to track the packets of information sent to and from a computer.

Password—A password is a personal code that the user selects to access their account with their ISP.

Personal Information—As it relates to identity theft, refers to information associated with an actual person or a fictitious person that is a name, an address, a telephone number, an electronic mail address, a driver's license number, a social security number, an employer, a place of employment, information related to employment, an employee identification number, a mother's maiden name, an identifying number of a depository account, a bank account number, a password used for accessing information, or any other name, number, or code that is used, alone or in conjunction with other information, to confirm the identity of an actual or a fictitious person.

Personally Identifiable Information (PII)—Refers to information such as name, mailing address, phone number or e-mail address.

Ping—A short message sent by a computer across a network to another computer confirming that the target computer is up and running.

Platform for Privacy Preferences Project (P3P)—A proposed browser feature that would analyze privacy policies and allow a user to control what personal information is revealed to a particular site.

Pose—As it relates to identity theft, means to falsely represent oneself, directly or indirectly, as another person or persons.

Preference Data—Data which may be collected by a site or a service provider about an individual's likes and dislikes.

Pretexting—The practice of fraudulently obtaining personal financial information, such as account numbers and balances, by calling financial institutions under the pretext of being a customer.

Pretty Good Privacy (PGP)—A widely used encryption software.

Private Key—A data file assigned to a single individual to use in decrypting messages previously encrypted through use of that person's key.

Privacy Policy—A privacy policy is a statement on a website describing what information about the user is collected by the site and how it is used; also known as a privacy statement or privacy notice.

Privacy Seal Program—A program that certifies a site's compliance with the standards of privacy protection. Only those sites that comply with the standards are able to note certification.

Proxy Server—A proxy server is a system that caches items from other servers to speed up access.

Pseudonymity—A situation in which the user has taken on an assumed identity.

Public Forum—Refers to a digital entity such as a bulletin board, public directory, or commercial CD-ROM directory, where personal user data may be distributed by a site or a service provider.

Public Key—A data file assigned to a specific person but which others can use to send the person encrypted messages. Because public keys don't contain the components necessary to decrypt messages, they are safe to distribute to others.

Query String—The extended string of a URL after the standard website address.

Remedy—The remedy is the means by which a right is enforced or a violation of a right is compensated.

Restitution—Restitution refers to the act of restoring a party to a contract to their status quo, i.e., the position the party would have been in if no contract had been made.

Screen Name—A screen name is the name the user selects to be known by when the user communicates online.

Search Engine—A search engine is a function that lets the user search for information and websites. Search engines or search functions may be found on many web sites.

Secondary Use—Refers to using personal information collected for one purpose for a second, unrelated purpose.

Secure Anonymous Remailer—Web sites that will strip a consumer's identifying information so they can surf other Web sites and send e-mail anonymously.

Server—A host computer that stores information and/or software programs and makes them available to users of other computers.

Spam—E-mail from a company or charity that is unsolicited and sent to many people at one time, usually for advertising purposes; also known as junk e-mail.

Static IP Address—An IP address that remains the same each time a user logs on or dials up a server.

Third Party Ad Server—Companies that put banner advertising on websites that are generally not owned by that advertiser.

Third Party Cookie—A cookie that is placed by a party other than the user or the Web site being viewed, such as advertising or marketing groups who are trying to gather data on general consumer use third party cookies.

Trace Route—The course that a packet travels across the Internet from one computer to another.

Tracker GIF—Electronic images, usually not visible to site visitors, that allow a Web site to count those who have visited that page or to access certain cookies; also known as a "Clear GIF".

TRUSTe—An online privacy seal program that certifies eligible websites, holding sites to baseline privacy standards. TRUSTe requires its licensees to implement certain fair information practices and to submit to various types of compliance monitoring in order to display a privacy seal on their websites.

Trustmark—An online seal awarded by TRUSTe to websites that agree to post their privacy practices openly via privacy statements, as well as adhere to enforcement procedures that ensure that those privacy promises are met.

Uniform Resource Locator (URL)—The address that lets the user locate a particular site. For example, http://www.ftc.gov is the URL for the Federal Trade Commission. Government URLs end in .gov and non-profit organizations and trade associations end in .org. Commercial companies generally end in .com, although additional suffixes or domains may be used as the number of internet businesses grows.

Unique Identifiers—Non-financial identifiers issued for purposes of consistently identifying the individual.

Upload—Copying or sending data or documents from one computer to another computer.

Use—Refers to the practice of collecting and using personal data internally, within the company or organization, for both administrative and marketing purposes.

User—An individual on whose behalf a service is accessed and for which personal data exists.

Verifiable Parental Consent—A type of parental consent obtained by a website to collect information from children under age 13 which must be verifiable, e.g., by written permission or a credit card number.

Victim—As it relates to identity theft, refers to any person who has suffered financial loss or any entity that provided money, credit, goods, services or anything of value and has suffered financial loss as a direct result of the commission or attempted commission of identity theft.

Virus—A virus is a file maliciously planted in the user's computer that can damage files and disrupt their system.

Waiver—Waiver refers to an intentional and voluntary surrender of a known right.

Web Bug—A graphic in a website or enhanced e-mail message that enables a third party to monitor who is reading the page or message.

Website—A website is an internet destination where the user can look at and retrieve data. All the web sites in the world, linked together, make up the World Wide Web or the "Web."

World Wide Web—A part of the Internet housing websites that provide text, graphics, video and audio information on millions of topics.

BIBLIOGRAPHY

Better Business Bureau On-Line (Date Visited: May 2003) <http://www.bbbonline.org>.

Black's Law Dictionary, Fifth Edition. St. Paul, MN: West Publishing Company, 1979.

Center for Democracy and Technology (Date Visited: May 2003) <http://www.consumerprivacyguide.org>.

Center for Media Education (Date Visited: May 2003) <http://www.cme.org>.

Consumer Information Center (Date Visited: May 2003) <http://www.pueblo.gsa.gov>.

Consumer Sentinel (Date Visited: May 2003) <http://www.consumer.gov/sentinel>.

CyberAngels (Date Visited: May 2003) <http://www.cyberangels.org>.

Direct Marketing Association (Date Visited: May 2003) <http://www.the-dma.org>.

Federal Bureau of Investigation Internet Fraud Complaint Center (Date Visited: May 2003) <http://www.ifccfbi.gov>.

Federal Deposit Insurance Corporation (Date Visited: May 2003) <http://www.fdic.gov>.

Federal Trade Commission (Date Visited: May 2003) <http://www.ftc.gov>.

Get Net Wise (Date Visited: May 2003) <http://www.getnetwise.org>.

Identity Theft Resource Center (Date Visited: May 2003) <http://www.idtheftcenter.org>.

National Consumer's League (Date Visited: May 2003) <http://natlconsumersleague.org>.

National Infrastructure Protection Center (Date Visited: May 2003) <http://www.nipc.gov>

Online Privacy Alliance (Date Visited: May 2003) <http://www.privacyallliance.com>.

Online Public Education Network (Date Visited: May 2003) <http://www.internetalliance.org>.

Privacy Leadership Initiative (Date Visited: May 2003) <http://www.understandingprivacy.org>

Privacy Rights Clearinghouse (Date Visited: May 2003) <http://www.privacyrights.org>.

Truste (Date Visited: May 2003) <http://www.truste.org>.

United States Department of Justice (Date Visited: May 2003) <http://www.usdoj.gov/criminal/fraud/idtheft.html>.

United States General Accounting Office (Date Visited: May 2003) <http://www.gao.gov>.

United States Office of the Attorney General (Date Visited: May 2003) <http://www.oag.gov>.

United States Secret Service (Date Visited: May 2003) <http://www.treas.gov/usss>.

United States Social Security Administration (Date Visited: May 2003) <http://www.ssa.gov>.

Wired Kids (Date Visited: May 2003) <http://www.wiredkids.org>.